TIPS & TRICKS FOR CAT OWNERS

BY HERTA PUTTNER, D.V.M.AND EVA ROHRER
TRANSLATED BY WILLIAM CHARLTON

COPYRIGHT

TABLE OF CONTENTS

TIPS & TRICKS FOR CAT LOVERS

CONTENTS

TABLE OF CONTENTS

A CAT ARRIVES IN THE HOME

More and more people are choosing a cat as a pet. Whether it is to combat loneliness, whether it is as a playmate for the children, or whether it is simply because they have taken these sensitive individualists to heart. As always — the cat has purred its way into our favor.

"Purred" into our hearts

Who is not delighted by the sight of a kitten meowing plaintively? More than one person has rashly taken in or given away a kitten, because it is "so sweet." Although life with a cat promises many pleasant hours, a few problems or troubles can turn up, which you failed to consider at the moment of your initial enthusiasm. Maybe you will have to change certain parts of your daily routine or do without something.

Do not be seduced

For that reason it is important that you know precisely the needs and behavior patterns of a cat, to avoid any "unpleasant surprises." You must be aware that lack of knowledge about the animal is one of the reasons why so many cats end up in animal shelters or, even worse, are abandoned. They often come to a bad end, if they are not lucky enough to be picked up by a new owner.

What do you know about cats?

5

A CAT ARRIVES IN THE HOME

Misconceptions

The keeping of cats is often underestimated. Keeping a cat requires even more ability to empathize than does keeping a dog. Misconceptions raise expectations in the owner, which the cat by nature cannot live up to. A cat simply cannot be kept like a dog.

They do not recognize subordination

The dog is a pack animal, which becomes attached to people and always loves its master and mistress, regardless of how it is treated. We must treat the cat with great care and understanding, so that it gives us affection. Cats are loners that do not recognize conformity, the pecking order, and the subordination in a pack. They would rather suffer psychic and physical injury, than to be forced to do something against their will. So, you see that this has nothing to do with defiance or stubbornness, as is often assumed of cats.

Cats learn by watching

Anyone who loves his or her cat will soon notice that a certain balance between the interests of the four-legged friend and the human being settles in. Experience has shown that the cat, when it has a good relationship with its owner, will submit to actions that it finds unpleasant. We can trace this back to the cat's ability for close observation. The cat plays with retracted claws and, for example, puts up relatively well with small children. This reflects a certain degree of adaptation. The cat will not, however, obey.

The human as

Scientists suspect that the reason the cat has bonded with humans at all is that it remains stuck in the childlike developmental stage. Mother cats in the wild drive away the young when they no longer find enough food and have too little milk. The young cat must become independent. With domestic cats, the human, so to speak, takes over the maternal role. If he or she does not push the cat away, the pussycat transfers its childlike affection to the owner.

maternal substitute

The majority of problems with cats in the home arise because they have too little stimulation and occupation, and in the owner's eyes "cause trouble" because they are bored. House cats cannot change their innate behavior. Therefore, the owner should create the necessary conditions for an interesting and varied life in the home. (See chapter "What the Cat Needs.")

Offer more variety

Above all, however, you need time to play and cuddle, although the cat determines the time and duration of any activity. It is a misconception to believe that the cat wants to be carried around and petted constantly. It is unpleasant for the animal when you try to force closeness. For working people, a second cat is beneficial for providing the necessary social contact for the cats.

The cat has the final say

Unlike somewhat larger dogs, cats can make do with the smallest home, as long as they have an interesting environment and a quiet place to sleep and do their business. Open room doors are important, so that the cat can roam about, a scratching

How much room does the cat need?

post, and people who treat the cat according to its nature.

***Are you
prepared?***   You cannot simply get rid of a living creature when you have grown tired of it. You must be prepared to assume responsibility, both financially and emotionally.

Cost   • You must be prepared to raise approximately $30 a month, and sacrifice a vacation if you have failed to make timely arrangements to find someone to take care of the cat.

• You must not take offense if the cat coughs up a hair ball, or vomits, or happens not to use its litter box.

• Does it disgust you to clean the litter box or to put up with the often intense smell of canned cat food?

• Do you dread the extra work of having to clean your house more often, because cats shed all year long?

• Can you get over it when the cat scratches on a piece of furniture, hangs from the drapes, prefers to sleep on your nicest sofa, or awakens you in the morning with loud meowing?

"Sacrifice"   True cat lovers are prepared to accept all of this and to make sacrifices, because for them the pleasure of the animal's company makes up for it. If this is not obvious to you, you really should carefully consider the wisdom of acquiring a cat.

Cats have fewer needs than dogs. Anyone who does not like to walk the dog in any weather is better off with a cat. You do not have to take them outside, because they do their business in the litter box. You can leave cats alone for a few hours without any problems, whereas a dog, for example, suffers terribly in this situation.

The good news

Cats are considered to be very clean animals, because they groom themselves intensively and have no odor of their own. They are very quiet, and we often do not notice them at all when they are around, because they like to sleep, rest, or watch. On the other hand, they also like to play with their owner.

Cats are very clean

We can keep cats even in very small homes, as long as we meet their requirements, such as a litter box, scratching post, and quiet places to eat and sleep. (We will discuss this topic in more detail in subsequent chapters.)

Touching is the most important contact between the human and the cat. The cat brushes its body against our legs and lovingly rubs its head on us. In turn, we readily pet it and scratch it under its chin. Experience has shown that frazzled owners relax and reduce stress in this way. For older people, as well, cats are the ideal pet, because they drive loneliness away and can be kept without great expense. — Soothing medicine for young and old!

Gentle companions

A CAT ARRIVES IN THE HOME

Which cat for which person

Although the differences between cats are not as great as those between dogs, we can divide them roughly into three personality types, although, of course, there are always exceptions to the rule. Keep in mind that young kittens, in particular, can turn out differently depending on the environmental conditions:

Calm cats

• Calm cats are balanced, and cat owners of the same personality type will enjoy their company. You can recognize a kitten of this temperament in a litter because it is good-natured toward its siblings. It approaches slowly and deliberately, but not timidly. With older cats, the following is true: they do not run away, to watch from a safe distance, but rather stay where they are.

Outgoing cats

• Anyone who seeks an outgoing, sociable cat of this kind should choose one that is not shy at all and soon approaches inquisitively and amiably and allows itself to be petted. Such animals also like to play and are therefore particularly suitable for children. Some daredevils among these cats take over the home from the first day on.

Reserved cats

• Some cats are reserved by nature. Furthermore, these cats are often the weakest of the litter and tend to be dominated by their siblings. This often makes them even more reserved. Adult cats often become timid and cautious because of bad experiences. Shy cats avoid direct contact for a long time.

Dealing with a shy cat requires much patience, but this is usually rewarded in the long run. The cat becomes particularly devoted (but only toward its owner) after it overcomes its fear. These cats take change or the loss of the owner particularly hard.

Pedigreed cats from breeders are not cheap. You must expect to pay approximately $500 and more. Do not, however, only be influenced by the appearance!

Pedigreed cats

• Pedigreed cats, apart from their typical outward appearance, also have a particular temperament. Therefore, not every cat is suitable for every person. Persians, for example, are very easygoing and calm cats. At the opposite pole are the extremely lively Siamese Cats, which need much contact with their owner.

Temperament

• The different breeds also require different amounts of care. As beautiful as long-haired cats are, some require daily brushing and combing!

Care

• Pedigreed kittens sometimes look completely different when they are fully grown. The color and markings can change. When you have fallen in love with a kitten, also take a look at the mother cat!

Kittens

• Therefore, get detailed information from reputable breeders before you make the— wrong—decision.

A CAT ARRIVES IN THE HOME

Pedigreed cat from a breeder

Make sure that you go to a reputable breeder! They have specialized in one breed and show a great interest in the well-being of their animals. They advise the prospective owner, have the kittens vaccinated and dewormed before they deliver them, and furnish the necessary documentation. Furthermore, reputable breeders allow you to see the kittens before you pick them up. In this way you can immediately get an idea about the keeping conditions and the development of the animals.

Is the cat healthy?

At first sight, the following characteristics distinguish an apparently healthy cat: The coat shines and feels soft, and has no thin bare, or inflamed spots. The eyes are neither filled with discharge nor inflamed, but rather clear and shiny. Healthy animals that feel well move gracefully and lithely.

Caution is advised

• If several breeds are offered: You could be dealing with a "kitten mill."

• Kittens from kitten mills are scarcely accustomed to people because of the lack of time or lack of love of animals. They also frequently get sick.

• If the seller does not treat the kitten as a living creature, but rather as a commodity.

• If you are not allowed to see the kittens before delivery, particularly the place where they are being raised.

• With newspaper advertisements: Such

advertisements are not only run by cat lovers who are trying to sell their kittens privately and want to find them good homes. Unfortunately, profit seekers, who do not have any real interest in cats, also try to sell their "goods" to make as much money as possible. The kittens usually are not vaccinated, have no papers or forged ones, and often are not healthy.

It does not have to be a pedigreed cat. Real animal lovers also take cats from animal shelters.

The animal shelter

Many absolutely want a kitten. Yet there are also reasons why an older animal has its advantages.

• If you are young and your life frequently changes both professionally and personally: Consider that with a kitten, you must count on at least 15 years of responsibility.

• If you work: You cannot leave a kitten alone at first. It requires much more attention. It is still very curious and active and "gets into everything."

• A younger, but fully grown (not shy) cat is particularly suitable for families with small children. The cat should be gentle and accustomed to social contact, because small children are sometimes still unruly. A good-natured adult cat withdraws from the children's grasp without scratching or biting. Never-

13

theless, you must teach the child how to handle the cat, or the animal will suffer if the children constantly attack it, scare it with loud shouting, or hunt it.

Why older cats?

• For older people, an older cat is also better suited, because it is no longer as boisterous and no longer needs constant attention and "control." The cat is usually already neutered, or the animal shelter can perform the operation cheaply.

Female or male?

It is said that females are generally more affectionate and loving, males more robust, more reserved, and "wilder." Many tomcats, or particularly independent females, have given the lie to this notion. There are problems with both when they reach sexual maturity. This occurs starting in about the fifth to seventh month with house cats, and somewhat later (ninth to twelfth month) with pedigreed cats.

Beware, sexual maturity!

When females are in heat, which can last one to three weeks, they screech and behave wildly. Males, on the other hand, mark the house with their urine, which has a terrible smell. To prevent these conditions in the home, and so as not to put the cats in misery, you should have the animals neutered (see chapter "Sexuality").

Indoor cat or

It is an old disputed issue, whether you should keep cats outdoors or only in the house. It is basically true that an outdoor cat is exposed to many dangers that are by no means "of natural origin." They are often run over, poisoned, shot by hunters, or end up in a trap.

outdoor cat?

If you let the cat outside, you should at least keep it in the house at night, because the most can happen during this time. In any case, female cats and tomcats should be neutered, to avoid the aforementioned problems in the house, as well as the unchecked propagation of the animals that live outdoors.

In the house at least at night

WHAT THE CAT NEEDS

Prepare ahead of time

When you have finally decided on a particular animal, whether a kitten or a member of the older generation, from an animal shelter or a breeder, you should not only prepare psychologically for the cat, but also furnish your household in a cat-friendly way. It is best to make a list ahead of time so that you do not forget anything.

A place to sleep

Put the cat basket in an undisturbed place, from where the cat can still watch (cats are sight animals). If you put a blanket in the bed for the cat to snuggle in, it will feel particularly comfortable. There are also covered cat beds, into which the cat can withdraw completely. The sleeping place should be free of drafts and warm. It can still happen, however, that the cat will not like the bed provided for it and will pick out its own favorite place to sleep.

Litter box

The litter box is very important. It is available in various styles as a simple plastic basin with a raised rim, or with a cover and drawer for changing the litter. Put the litter box in a protected place, which the cat has access to at all times.

Cat litter

Cat litter that reduces odors (make sure it

is free of asbestos) is available today. The feces and urine clump with a part of the litter and are easily scooped up and removed. Biological litter is also available on the market. It can be composted after the feces are removed.

Food and water dishes

The dishes should be as heavy as possible, to keep them from tipping over or sliding. Clay and porcelain dishes are well suited. Put the dishes on a plastic sheet, because cats "dribble" when they eat and drink. If you have a long-haired cat, shallow dishes are better suited. If you put the water dish away from the food bowl, the cat can "go to the water hole to drink," as its ancestors once did.

Scratching post spares the furniture

To keep your cat from attacking the furniture and carpet, provide it with a sturdy, large (the cat should be able to stand on its hind legs while scratching) board covered with hemp or thick linen. Mount it to a wall, a door post, the side of a cabinet.

Grass as a remedy for swallowed hair

Cats need vegetable matter to help them to vomit up the hair they swallow while grooming. Furthermore, cats also take up vitamins and minerals with it, which wild cats obtained from the partially digested plants filling the innards of the prey animals. Cats will also attack your house plants if no cat grass is available to them. Moreover, certain house plants are poisonous. You can obtain suitable grass on the market. You can, however, also offer your cat umbrella grass (with soft, flexible blades) or a pot of chives.

WHAT THE CAT NEEDS

Comb and brush
For short-haired cats, a nubbly rubber brush or a brush with fine natural bristles is suitable. For long-haired cats you need a brush with curved metal bristles as well as two metal combs, one with fine teeth and the other with coarse teeth.

Toys
Young kittens, in particular, are very fond of playing. Give them a fur mouse, small (but not too small!) hard rubber balls, empty boxes, crumpled newspaper, little rag dolls, wooden dowels, and so forth. Children's toys are usually unsuitable, because they could bite off and swallow parts of them.

Cat carrier
You absolutely need a cat carrier. Not only to pick up the cat, but also later when you take it, for example, to the veterinarian or you have to bring it with you somewhere. The best suited are heavy-duty carriers with locking gates. It is not sufficient to simply carry the cat in your arms or to put it in a bag. It could be frightened by something and jump away in panic. What this means, for example, in a neighborhood with heavy traffic or near a wood needs no further explanation here.

Cat harness and leash
Although you cannot lead a cat on a leash like a dog, it can nevertheless be helpful in certain situations to have a leash available. The cat harness not only goes around the neck, but around the chest and belly as well, to keep from choking the cat. If a cat is allowed outdoors, it should have a collar (with an elastic band, so that it does not get

caught on something and strangle the cat) with an address card.

As was previously mentioned, the size of the home is not decisive. What is important is whether it is interesting enough for the cat. Cats get bored and feel lonely when they are left alone too long in an uninteresting environment. Then they are more prone to "cause mischief" or exhibit behavioral disorders. The secret is variety.

Environ-ment suitable for cats

- Safe niches and hiding places lined with fabric. Climbing trees with "branches" and shelves to perch on at various heights, this is to give the cat the opportunity to clamber about.

- An observation post in a screened window or a screened balcony offers the opportunity to observe, which the cat is particularly fond of.

- A thick rope offers an excellent opportunity for exercise. Colorful ribbons and balls of aluminum foil to play with, paper sacks to hide in (cut off the handles beforehand, so that the cat cannot get its head caught), newspaper to rustle, boxes to hide in, and so on. Variety is important. Always offer your cat something new.

DANGERS FOR CATS

Chemicals   Store detergents, household cleaners, varnish, and the like in a cat-proof place. Also be careful when using them. If the cat walks across detergent powder, oil, or other chemicals on the floor, it will lick these off when it grooms its fur. Fertilizer spikes in flowerpots can be just as tempting to a cat as liquid fertilizer in the watering can.

Dangerous poisons   Be careful with insecticides, herbicides, pesticides, rat poison, antifreeze, and so forth! Should the cat be poisoned, immediately take it to the veterinarian. Never try to treat it yourself! Never administer milk to the cat! With certain poisons, the protein even intensifies the effect!

Do not leave anything lying around!   Do not leave anything lying around that the cat could taste or swallow, such as cigarette butts, medicines, or cosmetics. Put away pointed or sharp objects as well. Marbles and pearls could also be swallowed and suffocate the cat. The same applies to adhesive bandages, cigarette wrappers, remnants from handicrafts, and so forth.

Poisonous plants   Make sure that you have no poisonous house plants in the home. These include

20

dieffenbachia, philodendron, rubber tree, ivy, clivia, cyclamen, and poinsettia.

Kittens are also fascinated by electric cords. Many accidents with cats happen because of easily accessible cords. The cats bite through them or stick their claws in them and can suffer an electric shock or serious burns. Place or cover the cord so that the kitten cannot reach it. Hanging or drooping cords are particularly tempting.

Electric shock

Close off balconies and open windows with wire or nylon screens! Most cats fall from the balcony or windowsill from May to October. Two-thirds of the cats are less than three years old. Flies or the sight of a bird or butterfly can trigger the cat's play instinct, causing it to lean out too far.

Falls from windows

It is said of cats that they always land safely on their feet. Unfortunately, this is rarely true, and not true at all when the animal falls from a higher story. Otherwise, there would not be so many injured or even dead cats after such falls every year.

No "nine" lives

Do not leave plastic bags lying around, because the cat could crawl into them, get trapped, and suffocate. Also, do not leave drawers and cabinet doors open and then close them later. The cat could have made itself comfortable inside and could then be trapped.

Suffocated inside a plastic bag

Tilt-in windows are a dangerous trap. If you tilt the window, secure it with a special

The trap of the

tilt-in window   insert. Otherwise, should the cat happen to try to get through the unsecured crack, it could get caught and strangle itself or suffer serious injuries from the moving parts.

Danger, hot!   It is best to cover hot stove burners with a covered pot filled with cold water. Turn off irons when you leave the room.

Burning candles   Do not leave a cat unsupervised in a room with a burning candle. The cat could be frightened and might tip over the candle. Also, do not leave smoldering cigarettes in the ashtray.

Sewing needles and rubber bands   Make sure that you do not "lose" sewing needles on the floor. The cat could step on the needle or swallow it and injure itself. In general, when you are finished, always put away all sewing utensils, such as thread, buttons, hooks, snaps, and so forth. Store rubber bands out of reach, too.

The trap of the washing machine   Cats — whether large or small — always find hiding places attractive. Make sure that the cat has not hidden itself in the supposed hiding place of the washing machine before you turn it on. This is particularly true if you have already loaded the laundry as a "plush nest"!

Holes and shafts   Make sure to cover holes and shafts. Do not close sheds, garages, and so forth before you make sure that the cat is not inside.

THE CAT IS HERE

Kittens should stay with their mother at least eight weeks, preferably twelve, to learn all the important things they will need to know for the rest of their lives: social rules of the game, grooming, how to use the litter box, and so forth.

How long with the mother?

When the time has come and you have made all your preparations, pick up your future companion in a securely closed cat carrier, preferably in a car. Ask a family member or a friend to come with you to talk reassuringly to the cat during the trip. Drive slowly and carefully.

You pick up the cat

Put the carrier in a quiet place near the litter box and the food and water dishes. Then open the door. (You should bring the same food that the cat was used to.) Ask the previous owner about all particulars when you pick up the cat. At most lure out the animal quietly and calmly by calling its name, but never remove it by force. It must first recover from the shock of the trip and the strange environment. With kittens you must also take into account the stress of separation from the mother and siblings.

The new home

After a while the cat will emerge inquisitively, but will still cower and creep cautiously along the wall. Then it will probably hide under a sofa, table, or cabinet. Give it time to get used to the new home gradually. It will leave its hiding place when it feels safe and realizes that it has nothing to be afraid of.

House-breaking

Housebreaking is no problem with cats, unless behavioral disorders are present, or the cat is exposed to change (see the pertinent chapter). Cats are models of cleanliness. They groom themselves frequently, and once you have shown them the litter box cats, will also use it. Put the litter box in a quiet, protected place and fill it with several centimeters of cat litter.

At the right moment

You can help a young kitten to use the litter box if it does not yet do so on its own. Watch the kitten. When it meows, looks inside the litter box somewhat helplessly and expectantly, and then scrapes at the floor, it is announcing that it is ready to relieve itself. Then it crouches, spreads its legs slightly, and raises its tail. This is the moment to put it in the litter box immediately. If it now urinates or defecates, praise and stroke it immediately.

Keep it clean!

You must always keep the litter box clean. Some cats will not even use it twice. Therefore, remove feces and wet litter regularly with a small scoop. This is very easy today, because special litter clumps readily with the urine and is easy to remove. Then add a little more litter.

You should change the cat litter completely once a week. It does not belong in the toilet, but in a plastic bag in the trash! Rinse out the litter box with hot water and wipe it dry. Do not use dishwashing liquid or other cleanser, because the odor could keep the cat from using the litter box again.

Change every week

ACCLIMATION

Regularity It is best to maintain a consistent daily routine from the start. The first step, of course, is the acclimation to the litter box. You should also feed and groom the cat at set times.

Accustom the cat to its name immediately Naturally, you should accustom a cat to its name immediately. While feeding, grooming, and petting the cat, always repeat its name, and very soon it will readily answer to it, particularly, of course, at feeding time.

Cats are sensitive When dealing with your cat, avoid noise, wild movements, commotion, and harsh words. Cats are very sensitive and after such experiences often remain distrustful and shy for a long time!

Trust is everything You must give the cat time to learn to trust you. Initial impatience by the owner has caused many setbacks here. Avoid the most common mistakes:

- Never approach the cat quickly or run after it and pick it up from above. Absolutely do not sneak up on it from behind and pick it up.

- When you want to make contact with your cat, call to it softly by name. When you reach it, it will crane its neck forward and sniff at you. Hold your position and continue to talk.

Approach cautiously

- Then you can slowly extend your hand, and first stroke the cat with a finger. If it puts up with this, you can now stroke it with your whole hand. Always extend your hand at the level with the cat's head, so that it can see it.

Hold out your hand

- If the cat is very shy, do not stroke it at first. Instead, hold out a treat suitable for cats to it and allow it to sniff or lick it. In doing so it will also eventually touch your hand. It will notice that nothing has happened and will get accustomed to it.

Treats for shy cats

TEACHING & BAD HABITS

Teaching, but how?

You cannot, of course, teach a cat in the sense of training it. Any attempt of this kind will, at most, cause behavioral disorders. To a certain degree, however, you can break the animal of bad habits or accustom it to certain "rules of behavior." More frequently, it is actually the owner who must change certain things to avoid teaching the cat bad habits.

Several important measures in teaching

If you have a family, all members should agree about what the animal should do, may do, and may not do. Only in this way will the cat be able to get its bearings. If each person permits or forbids something else, the cat will feel unsure and ultimately will develop a behavioral disorder.

• Always speak in a calm tone of voice to your cat. If it trusts you, it will be more likely to do what you want.

Teaching measures

• Do not get nervous if everything does not succeed straight off. Cats react particularly sensitively to anxiety.

• Do not force anything if your cat does not happen to show any desire to learn something new.

- Avoid hectic movements, even friendly ones; the cat could misunderstand.

- When you want to teach the kitten something, never practice more than a half hour a day. Repeat any exercise only a few times, or the kitten will become annoyed and may not "learn" anything at all.

- Very deep and very high voices can throw the cat into a state of panic. When you praise the cat, it is best to speak in a low tone of voice. When you want to scold, speak somewhat more loudly, but not shrilly!

- If you want to forbid something, always do so consistently. With begging at the table, for example, the cat will not understand "sometimes yes and sometimes no." Once it is allowed to have something, it will always want it.

- A quick, surprising squirt from a water pistol or a plant sprayer, when you catch the cat in the act, has brought many cats to reason. (The animals should not, however, know where the water came from.)

- One rule always applies in teaching: surprise instead of pain (never hit the animal). Put dry beans in a pot and shake it briefly and vigorously if your cat happens to be hanging from the drapes. Do not shout, however, or the cat will associate the unpleasantness with you and not with the deed.

Teaching measures

29

- Always use the same expression for bans and commands; for example, a short, definite "No" or "Bad."

- When the cat obeys, you should praise and stroke it.

- Another good trick for teaching is the "more food method": Have the cat's normal food available, its favorite food, and a special delicacy or treat. If the cat responds to you and follows the teaching lesson, give it a little of the normal food. If it makes a special effort, give it some of its favorite food. If it turns in a fantastic performance, give it the treat. Do not, however, reward with food too often! Do not forget stroking and praise.

- Shouting and hitting do not help with "bad" cats. Usually, you only achieve the opposite of what you intended, or the animal becomes neurotic.

- Do not be "insulting" by ignoring your cat when you get mad at it. The cat will not understand this and will feel insecure.

- Do not scare the cat. Fear ruins any attempt to teach.

Scratching on furniture
The cat does not always know from the start that it may only use the scratching board or tree to sharpen its claws. Then you must teach it to scratch in the proper place.

If the cat begins to "attack" the furniture, correct it with a clear "No" or "Out." Then immediately take the cat to a suitable place, and put the front paws on the scratching surface. You can also move the paws up and down or demonstrate it yourself. If you scratch with your own nails, the noise will make the cat curious. You will need patience to succeed.

Scratching sounds arouse curiosity

If the cat cannot be convinced at all to use the scratching board or tree, it may not like the covering. Try the following: Hang an old piece of clothing that carries your scent over the board, wind a thick hemp rope around the scratching tree, or put out a few straw mats, which cats often accept readily. If it still continues to attack the furniture, your only choice is a squirt of water from the plant sprayer (see above).

If it is stubborn

The cat's sleeping place should be quiet and as comfortable as possible, so that it will readily use it. A covered cat basket with a soft lining fulfills these wishes the best. The cat can retreat into the safety of the basket, while still being able to watch everything.

Comfortable cat bed

Once a cat has gotten accustomed to begging, you have little chance of ever breaking it of the habit. Unfortunately, many of us give in to the pitiful meowing animals, when they look at us with imploring eyes. These are the most frequent mistakes that make it so hard to keep cats away from our dinner table:

The cat begs

How to prevent begging

- Never anthropomorphize cats, no matter how sweet we find them to be, only because we like to have them around us. This encourages begging.

- Never offer the cat something from the dinner table.

- Never give treats outside of the feeding times, just because it "pleads so insistently."

- Never take the cat on your lap while eating at the dinner table, or immediately after.

- Accustom the cat to set feeding times.

- Preferably, give the cat its food at the same time as you are eating, but in its place and in its food dish. Even if you feed it before you eat, you will not be successful. Then the cat will quickly eat all its food and will come to watch anyway, to see if something falls to the floor.

- If the cat jumps onto your lap or hops on a chair next to you, correct it with a clear, definite "No," and put it down in the "cat place," or at some distance from the table.

Owner as scratching tree

If your cat uses you as a "scratching tree," or sucks or pulls at your clothing, tap it on the nose with your finger tip. Cats also do this amongst themselves. Use this method, however, only when the cat does something that you find unpleasant directly to your person.

If the cat nibbles on your house plants despite the availability of cat grass or chives, place mothballs (which must be out of reach of children because they are poisonous!) in the flowerpot. Cats hate this smell and will avoid the plants.

Nibbles on house plants

If the cat does its business alongside the litter box, lay out aluminum foil in the area, and leave only a narrow access to the litter box. The foil is unpleasant to the cat's paws. This will teach it to use the litter box.

Does its business alongside the litter box

You want to go to sleep, but your cat has no plans to go to bed, and races full of energy through the house. Were it not already the third night with the cat show . . . This is how to quiet your pussycat:

Bed time — but not for the cat...

- Late in the evening give it a little snack, to fill the belly and to bring the activity to a halt.

- If the cat is too chubby for an evening snack, give it a little less at its main meal, to save some for the snack.

- If the pussycat sleeps in the evening, wake it with its favorite game, so that it can romp around. Otherwise it will release its energy precisely when you want to go to sleep.

- A catnip toy would also work. The minty smell, which the cat downright "goes wild for," also makes it extremely active for a while, after which it will have to rest.

Good cat turns into a "devil" When the gentle cat suddenly "freaks out," goes wild, races through the house, bites and hisses, the owner is naturally horrified and totally baffled. Yet it is not rare at all for an angelic pussycat to turn into a "devil." This can have many causes:

• The cat has remained "stuck" in the juvenile phase. In general, cats living with people frequently exhibit juvenile behavior. Sometimes, however, it is particularly pronounced. This can be a sign that the young kitten lost its mother and siblings too early, and, therefore, is not used to being put in its place.

• Sometimes cats behave "childishly" out of boredom. You are, no doubt, familiar with "kneading," which has the purpose of stimulating the flow of milk in the mother's teats.

• Gentle biting can be an invitation to play, and cats also use their claws on each other. Cat skin and fur, however, protects against serious injuries. Human beings, however, lack this protection, and the teeth and claws can be rather painful.

Measures You can try the following if your cat has gone "wild":

• If you suspect that the cat is "cracking

up" out of boredom, because it is mostly alone at home, a second cat, thus a partner that understands it, would be ideal.

• Do not force your attention on the cat when it does not feel like doing anything. It could then react crossly. Naturally, it is also your right to turn the pussycat away when it wants to cuddle at a particularly inopportune moment. With a quiet, but definite "No," put the cat back on the floor.

• Cats take a particular route in the house, which they use again and again. Pay attention to this when you, for example, rearrange the furniture. Do not put the valuable antique in front of its nose, which it then might "work over" thoroughly.

• When you, for example, buy new furniture or refurbish old furniture, the cat will without fail come to terms with the "novelty." Therefore, you should watch your fellow-lodger for a whole day, to see how it accepts the changed situation. You should handle new objects intensively, so that your smell predominates and the cat is not stimulated even to mark because of the strange smells of chemicals and other humans.

It is instinctive for cats to hunt anything that moves. Some cats passionately like to catch birds and bring them to their owner to be praised, because they be-

The cat catches birds

lieve that they have done something good. It certainly is not easy to break the cat's habit of catching birds. Try to do it as follows:

Measures

- If the cat strolls up with a bird in its mouth, stay calm and take the poor victim carefully out of the cat's mouth. If the bird can still fly, give it its freedom in the clear view of the cat, and show your cat in a stern tone of voice with appropriate comments that you no longer want such "presents." If the bird is dead, also show your displeasure to your cat, and remove the prey immediately (do not let your cat play with it!).

- Avoid feeding the cat for a short time after you have taken its prey away. Otherwise, it could think that it is being rewarded. You also must not pet it or spoil it in any other way.

- Watch your cat more closely for a while. If it shows by its behavior that it has set its sights on the next bird, again speak to it in a displeased tone of voice and possibly clap your hands to ruin its plans.

- It is a mistake to believe that the cat will not hunt on a full stomach. On the contrary, when it is hungry, a cat that is fed regularly will not make a great effort to catch its food. If you give it only a little to eat, it will soon return from its stroll to get the rest of its meal.

• If you find a nest in a tree, tie a strip of cloth around the trunk and spray it with cat repellent. You can also cut half the radius of the trunk from each of two fairly large boards, join them around the trunk and fasten them, so that the cat cannot climb higher.

• In persistent cases hang a small bell around the cat's neck to warn birds.

PLAY WITH THE CAT

To relieve boredom

Play is extraordinarily important for cats, particularly for house cats. In play, they practice the behavior and movements they need to hunt. In the home, play replaces stalking, attacking, jumping, and escaping. If it cannot play, the cat will be bored to death and waste away.

Play when it wants to

Play regularly with your pussycat — naturally, only when it signals to you its desire to do so. Evening is the best time, because cats are most active then. We have previously described how to furnish the home in an interesting way. Here are a few more tips for games that your cat will certainly enjoy:

• Roll a marble in the bathtub.

• Put your empty shopping bag or a box on the floor, where the cat can settle in. Tie a string to one of its toys and swing it inside. In this way the old toy will become interesting again.

• Do not throw the next cork from your wine bottle in the trash; instead, roll it through the house for the cat.

- Some cats will even play "fetch." Toss a little ball of aluminum foil or some other small toy to the cat. When it has the opportunity, it will bring you the "prey." When you want to end the game, distract the pussycat with something else, or simply leave the room.

- Hang a toy on the scratching tree and swing it back and forth, so that the cat jumps after it.

- Some cats also like to play hide-and-seek. It is best to begin by following the cat to a piece of furniture. While the cat is hiding behind the piece of furniture, go to another room, hide yourself, and call the cat to you. This will spur on the pussy cat to follow you. Then remain quiet until the cat has found you. Praise it and prepare as if to chase it. Wait a short time, until the pussycat is gone, and then look for it.

- Put all the toys in a small basket or box, so that the cat can fish them out as it likes.

TYPICAL CAT

How does the cat spend the day?

Have you ever thought about how a house cat spends the day?

- It sleeps for 16 hours,

- it grooms its coat for 5 hours,

- it rests or roams the house for 1 to 2 hours,

- it plays and "does gymnastics" for 15 minutes,

- it spends only about 10 minutes eating.

Cats that must catch their own food still sleep a great deal, to gather energy for the hunt. Yet, house cats spare themselves the trouble of catching prey, and still "sleep an extra round."

The marvel of the cat's body

You could describe the cat as a technical masterpiece. With its perfect interplay of bones, muscles, and joints, it achieves true supreme performance. For example, in jumping (about 11 feet high and up to 15 times its body length long), climbing, and balancing. When you watch the pussycat grooming itself, you can only envy its flexibility.

Cats can move very slowly and with great concentration when they stalk prey and spend a long time in ambush. When they are threatened by a dog, for example, they dash away at full speed from a standing start, although they cannot maintain their speed for long.

On the hunt

When the four-legged friend climbs a tree, it jumps up the first section, then digs its claws into the bark, and continues up the tree in this way. It sometimes happens to kittens that they miscalculate and climb too high. Then they sit in a fork of the tree and meow plaintively. Thus, many pussycats have had to be freed from its precarious situation by its owner or even the fire brigade. It is not as easy to go down as it is to go up. It cannot dig in its claws, and slides more than it climbs, because the claws of course, are rearward curving and therefore do not provide a foothold.

Going up is easy

If a pussycat is startled, it jumps back with all four legs simultaneously. If it wants to jump off a box, it bends well forward, to shorten the distance, Then pushes off to provide enough room for the hind legs to be able to land safely. The tail acts here as the "steering wheel." Beyond that, you can also tell the cat's mood by the tail posture.

The tail steers

The cat's coat protects the skin and regulates fluctuations in temperature. When the pussycat raises its hair, this is how the cat shows fear as well as threatens.

The coat — the universal garment

41

Cats very frequently lick at their coats, which they do not just for the sake of cleanliness. Licking also serves to keep the hair soft and supple, to provide better insulation from heat or cold. If it is very hot, they spread saliva over the coat, to cool themselves through evaporation, since cats have sweat glands only on the paws.

It notices only what moves

The eyes, ears, and whiskers are the most important sensory organs of the cat. Who is not fascinated by the big, beautiful eyes of the cat? They provide the cat with a panoramic view, without having to move the head. The cat only notices, however, things that move. As a predatory animal, it is programmed to do this. Within a range of six meters, the cat can make out even small insects — assuming that they move.

Nothing escapes it, even at night

The eyes of the cat are equipped such that the cat can get by with a fraction of the light that a human being requires to see. Furthermore, the cat can open its pupils much wider, to be able to gather even the smallest ray of light. During the day, the pupils become very narrow slits. Thus, when we can barely perceive anything more in the darkness, the cat can still see superbly.

Listen, listen!

As hunters, cats have an excellent sense of hearing. They can detect even very high-pitched and soft sounds, which we cannot hear — even the pattering of the tiny feet of a mouse. To pinpoint the sound, cats can move their ears independently of each other.

The whiskers are fine sensors, which the cat uses to detect objects with them, for example, it "measures" in the dark whether it will fit through a hole in the fence. The whiskers guide them around every obstacle and even protect the eyes, because every time they are touched, the blink reflex is triggered. **Sensitive whiskers**

Cats paint a picture of their environment with their nose. They have an additional organ, which makes it possible for them, so to speak, to smell and taste at the same time. In so doing the cat stands, stretches its head forward, and opens its mouth slightly. Cats send scent signals to one another (they have special glands on the head, chin, and near the anus), which we humans cannot detect (except for the unmistakable smell of unneutered tomcats). Cats are very sensitive to smells. Should your four-legged friend ever surprisingly avoid you, maybe the pussycat does not like the perfume of its mistress. Incidentally, cats also show their mood by the posture of the whiskers (see "What the cat is trying to say"). **A matter of taste**

People who do not like cats at all are often surprised that, of all people, the pussycat happens to pick their lap to jump onto. The cat does this precisely because the person shows no interest. If, on the other hand, you approach a strange cat and stare at it, it will regard this as an attack and run away. If you want to win the affection of a cat, ignore it. If you must look at the cat, then only do so from the side, never directly in the eyes. **Making friends with cats**

When the cat is shy

Avoid staring at the cat here as well. Crouch down so that you do not tower over it. Yawn and blink, which in cat language are signs of friendly intentions. Do not try to stroke the cat. Instead, wait until the pussycat rubs against you.

Why the scratching post is important

The scratching post is important in the first place, of course, to protect your furniture and other furnishings. There also are other important reasons, however, which lie in the nature of the cat:

• They must sharpen their claws regularly. In the process the old, uppermost layer of the claws is stripped off.

• For the cat in the wild, it is essential to test and train the extending and retracting mechanism, to be able to climb safely, catch prey, and fend off rivals.

• They want to demonstrate their dominance when other cats are in the vicinity.

Why they sit behind the curtains

Many animal owners ask themselves why cats (but dogs too) like to sit behind curtains and look through or under them. Behavioral researchers describe this as the so-called "corner effect." The cats like the feeling of protection from the two sides of a corner, or wall or glass and curtains. Furthermore, the animals simultaneously have a good, protected vantage point for watching what goes on both outside and inside the house when they sit in front of the balcony door or the window.

As an independent animal, which the cat happens to be, it can be tender and affectionate — when it wants to be — and the next moment give you the cold shoulder, or react with annoyance when something does not agree with it.

Understanding the cat

This is why some people unjustly accuse them of being devious. The cat shows, above all with its body, what kind of mood it is in and what it wants to say. It supports these gestures with various vocalizations. The human must first understand its language.

As mentioned previously, cats are very clean animals and usually use the litter box without any problems. Nevertheless, sudden elimination problems are common. This is no whim or vice on the part of the cat, and can have many causes. An unhousebroken cat is an unhappy cat. If the litter box is not accepted or is suddenly refused after long-term use, the cat is trying to say something to us. So, we must get to the root of the matter.

Help, the cat is not housebroken!

• The litter box is unsuitable

Causes

• Sexual maturity/marking

• The cat is sick or old (see chapter "Is my cat sick?")

• Changes

• The place where you put the litter box should be quiet, undisturbed, not too well lit, and as far away from the food dish as possible. Cats hate having to eat where they do their business. For this reason, it also helps to put the food dish where it is not supposed to do its business, and you should also leave it there when it is empty. If the causes are of a psychological nature, however, it will at most relieve itself in another place.

• Try a second litter box. Some cats urinate and defecate in separate places. Some refuse to use the litter box a second time, because a previously used litter box is offensive to them.

• If you have two cats, you need two litter boxes. Sometimes both cats use one litter box. Then, however, you must clean it frequently!

• It is repeatedly observed that cats, shortly before the owner leaves, quickly use the litter box one more time, so that he or she can remove the feces. On the other hand, other owners wonder why the litter box has not been used yet when they come home. Immediately after the owner's arrival, the cat uses the litter box, so that the owner can clean it immediately.

Behavior in the litter box

• Cats also refuse to use their litter box when they smell that you have cleaned the box with a cleansing or disinfecting agent. With healthy cats, use only hot water and wipe it dry.

- Cats scrape before "doing their business." If they do not do this or shake their paws afterward, they do not like the litter. Try a different brand.

- For former outdoor cats, which are to be acclimated to the house or the apartment, sand is better as a transition, because it resembles the natural conditions more closely. Gradually add wood shavings or shredded cellulose wadding, later cat litter, which finally replaces the sand.

- It can also be helpful to bury a piece of cellulose wadding or fabric dunked in cat urine, to show the cat the function of the litter box.

- If the cat has soiled the house, clean the spot with soap and a little club soda. Cover the spot or spray it with lemon oil, which most cats dislike. Do not use cleansing agents that contain ammonia. Ammonia contains aromatic essences that resemble urine! This encourages the cat to urinate again in the same place.

Sexual maturity

Female cats go in heat in the spring at three-week intervals, for a week at a time. At this time many urinate outside the litter box, presumably to attract males. Many sexually mature house cats also urinate in this way.

With sexually mature cats, you must also expect the spraying of urine with both

47

Marking female and male cats. When they spray the cats do not scrape beforehand or sniff at it afterwards, but rather spray a stream of urine. The reason for this is not precisely known. Apparently the sexually active cats mark their territory and thereby intend to "send a message."

Do not punish With housebreaking problems, punishment does not help. It is the natural instinct of the cat, which you cannot suppress. Neutering is the only solution in either case. Even neutered tomcats continue to spray occasionally to defend their territory when a new cat arrives, or if several cats live in the same home.

Confused by change Very often, changes are the reason for sudden problems. Any change in the daily routine or to the accustomed environment is unpleasant for the cat:

- Renovating the home, or rearranging the furniture. The removal of a piece of furniture that the cat was fond of. Installing new furniture.

- When doors in rooms to which the cat formerly had access are suddenly closed. The cat now instinctively wants to guard its smaller territory.

- If a strange person is staying in the house, whom the cat objects to, the cat may defecate in front of his or her door, or on the bed. This is not a malicious act by the cat, either. It is only trying to strengthen its rights to the house. (Self-confident cats also leave their feces uncovered at the borders of their territory, whereas timid cats bury them.)

Maybe you have acquired a new cat, and the old-established cat shows who's the "master of the house" by defecating or urinating outside the litter box.

Jealousy

- Or a baby enlarges the family and now your cat is jealous. The arrival of noisy children scares it. Give your cat more attention so that it does not feel neglected.

- If you punish the cat for an elimination problem, you will at most achieve the opposite result. The best way to accustom the cat to new situations is through much patience and attention.

Many animal owners believe that the cat is vicious if it bites during play. You must, however, make a distinction:

The cat is aggressive

- Kittens and cats living in the wild like to play, but they often do so very roughly. When cats play with each other, they also bite and scratch each other a little. They are protected from injury, however, by the coat. Not so with the skin of humans. When the kitten clasps the hand and bites, it can hurt a bit. No bad intentions, however, are behind it.

- Do not draw your hand back too quickly, because in this way you will only hurt yourself worse. And do not hit the cat. To the cat this would mean an attack in the middle of playing. From your behavior, however, the cat can understand that it has hurt you. If you, for instance, say loudly, "Ouch, that hurts," and show the cat the place it has bitten or scratched, as a sensitive animal the cat will understand this and will definitely be more careful.

If it bites you on the legs

Some cats have the habit of jumping on passers-by and biting their legs. Behavior researchers trace this back to an unsatisfied hunting and prey instinct and lack of activity. In this case you should spend more time with the cat and play with it (with objects that you move back and forth). Also try the following: Tie a toy to your leg with thread. As you walk by, the cat will be distracted from the leg by the toy.

Biting out of fear

Cats that have suffered bad treatment, and are neurotic and nervous, because they had to/must live with such people, can bite out of fear. In particularly flagrant cases, even very loving people will not be able to break down completely the fear and mistrust of the animal.

The newcomer is rejected

If a second cat comes into the house, it can happen that the old-established cat will reject the newcomer. Before the two engage in a wild fight, it is best to put the cats in separate rooms for a few days. Change the rooms every day. In this way each cat will become accustomed to the other's scent. Before you put the two together, open the door only a small crack and secure it so that the cats cannot get through. This gives them the opportunity to see and sniff each other. Only then should you attempt a supervised encounter.

If the aforementioned methods do not work, try it with a "peace bath." Bathe both cats and put them side by side afterwards. They will be so occupied with grooming and working on their coat that they will normally bury the hatchet, and even groom each other.

A bath for peace

When you have two cats that get along wonderfully, it can still happen that one animal suddenly rejects or even attacks the other. This is especially alarming to the owner. It can be that the cat that was attacked had changed its behavior, without the owner having noticed it. Cats, however, react to the slightest change.

The friend is rejected

Maybe the rejected one is sick and thereby is excited or behaves somewhat differently than usual. Maybe it creeps away or threatens the other because it is in pain or does not feel well. In this way, the formerly good friendship turns into hostility. Then you should separate the animals until the old conditions return; that is, the cat is healthy again, and so forth. There are, of course, exceptions as well: Some sick cats also trigger care behavior in other cats.

Separate and wait

My territory

Territorial fights in the wild are a natural instinctive behavior, and can only be prevented by keeping the cat indoors.

Fights between tomcats

Fights between sexually mature tomcats are also natural, but can be stopped immediately through neutering.

Why neuter?

- Neutering is absolutely necessary for reasons of animal protection. Imagine this: One pair of cats, if allowed to breed undisturbed, would produce approximately 80 million descendants in ten years! Countless cats populate animal shelters and many stray cats produce more offspring.

- Neutering also has benefits for the owner: The tomcat is unbearable in the home because of the intense smell. It marks its territory by spraying. If it is allowed outside, it stays away for many days, and often returns home emaciated and injured. The neighbors will be angry if it, say, marks the vegetable garden. If you have it neutered, it will no longer roam as far, it will give you more attention — but, as many fear incorrectly, it will not give up catching mice.

- Neutering is also better for the cat itself: In densely populated areas there are so many cats that the territories overlap, which puts additional stress on the tomcat and causes it to get into many more fights than would usually develop.

Not just humans can suffer from a "morbid craving for food," cats can too! Obese cats must be examined to see if organic diseases (metabolic disorders, such as diabetes) are to blame. *Craving for food*

If no organic disorders exist, the craving for food in cats is a serious behavioral disorder. Single cats that are kept indoors exclusively and have too little to do are particularly susceptible. *Eating out of boredom*

With the good intentions of doing everything for the cat, some owners always leave food available for their pussycat. Eating is often the only diversion in their boring feline existence and ultimately becomes the focus of their lives.

If you put the overweight cat on a diet, it will constantly follow you around and whine and cry for food, which is nerve-wracking for both parties and probably will eventually become unbearable. *Fewer calories, more exercise*

It is best to give your pussycat a greatly reduced-calorie diet under veterinary supervision. At the same time, however, you must fight the cause of the craving for food: Spend more time with the cat, play with it, and offer it a varied environment in the home for playing and climbing.

As a result of psychological shock, cats can completely lose their appetite and become anorexic. This is usually the case when they are separated from the owner or have to go to the animal shelter or kennel. This *Anorexia due to shock*

53

abates after the animal's situation has stabilized again. Fructose injections by the veterinarian help to stimulate the appetite.

The cat does not groom itself

Because cats are extremely fond of grooming themselves thoroughly, it is an alarm signal when they neglect this favorite pastime. If this is the case, the cat either is already very old, seriously ill, or suffers from an illness of the tongue. Then you must intervene. If grooming is neglected, the coat becomes so matted that you will have to cut out the hair mats. Suitable for this purpose is a coarse-toothed comb, which you must insert carefully between the mat and skin. Then cut out the "snarl" carefully with rounded scissors. The veterinarian must remove severe hair mats (see chapter "Care").

Excessive grooming

Excessive grooming and constant licking is also a sign that something is out of order. The usual causes are parasites, allergies, ringworm, or hormonal disorders (see chapter "Is my cat sick?").

The cat drools

Some cats drool, which seems "abnormal" to animal owners. To set your mind at rest, the increased flow of saliva can occur both with unpleasant and joyful excitement.

Nursing and kneading

You should not be upset when cats nurse on pieces of clothing or your finger and at the same time knead with their front paws (kittens do this with the mother, to stimulate the flow of milk). This means that they have remained stuck in their juvenile phase. It is also a sign of affection when the cat kneads with the front paws.

A cat must climb and jump. It will not want to stay only on the floor. Therefore, it will make its rounds in the house on chairs, sofas, and cabinets. Anyone who tries to deny the cat this variety and opportunity to explore, drives the pussycat into psychological disorders.

Mountain climbers and jumpers

If you do not want the cat to jump on the bed, you must always close the bedroom door. It will want to jump on the table, too. This is one piece of furniture, however, that you can keep it off (for methods, see chapter "Training, Bad Habits"). Another solution is simply to close the dining room door after you have set the table.

Jumps on the bed or table

MOVING WITH THE CAT

The cat does not like change   Cats are attached to their territory and are not fond of change. If the cat has a good relationship with you, it will cope with the move more easily with your help.

• First clear out one room, and keep the cat with its sleeping basket, toys, litter box, etc. only in this room until you finish. In this way, you will spare the cat at least from some of the commotion of moving.

• Again put the cat (in a locked cat carrier) in the new home in an empty room with its things.

• Only after everything is in place in the home, gradually accustom the pussycat to its new home. Talk quietly to it, and give it time to explore the new territory. Show the cat the new place for the food and water dishes and the litter box.

• If the cat is allowed outside, avoid this, at least in the beginning, until it has become acclimated to the new home and does not try to run away. For safety's sake, give it a collar with a tag that gives its new address.

DOGS AND CATS TOGETHER

There are very few exceptions where the dog and cat cannot get used to each other at all. It is frequently the case that cats and dogs become close friends and even sleep snuggled together in the dog's bed. The cat, in particular, seeks out the warmth. Whether enmity or friendship prevails between the dog and cat depends largely on how you bring the two together.

Can you keep dogs and cats together?

Misunderstandings can occur, however, at least in the beginning, because the dog and cat have different, in some cases even opposing, behavior patterns for expressing something, to put it mildly. Dogs are hunters, but cats want to play, and this can occasionally lead to minor misunderstandings.

Why misunderstandings occur

Breeds with a stronger hunting instinct, such as terriers, which once were bred exclusively as hunters, find it more difficult to get along with cats than do herding or working dogs.

Finding it harder to adjust

As long as you proceed carefully and prepare the animals well for each other, it makes no difference who was first the "master of the house."

Who first: the dog or the cat?

Less of a problem: kittens and puppies

Puppies and kittens naturally get accustomed to each other with the fewest problems. An adult cat or an adult dog also accepts the other best in the juvenile stage. A puppy that has become acquainted with cats at a very early age will no longer view them as welcome prey throughout its life.

Cautious approach

Proceed cautiously and very calmly with the first encounter between your pet and the new fellow lodger. The new pet should stay in one room at first. Your "old" friend should have the opportunity to approach and see the newcomer first. Do not put the two four-legged friends face to face. This leads to tension, fear, or aggression.

Adjust them while they sleep

Dogs and cats should get acquainted with each other without fear or threats. The best way to do this is by the sense of smell. Put something that smells like the dog in the cat's basket and an object with the cat's smell in the dog's sleeping place.

Do not leave them unsupervised!

Do not leave the two unsupervised in the beginning. A temporary quiet does not necessarily mean that the fronts have been settled. Watch for agitation, fear, or threat displays with the four-legged friends. It is best to distract them with food. Put the dog and cat in the same room, but far apart. In this way the two are distracted, but still smell the other and associate with each other the pleasant act of eating. You must expect it to take a few weeks for the four-legged friends to get used to each other.

No matter how big the dog is, by nature the cat assumes the position of "boss" — as it also ultimately does in relation to the owner. In this respect, size is not of decisive importance. Only very rarely does this pecking order not become established. Should this happen, large dogs are, of course, more dangerous.

Are large dogs more dangerous?

Cats usually threaten dogs by raising their hair and hissing. Occasionally they also slap the dog a few times. This in itself is not serious. The situation becomes ticklish only when the cat is frightened and timid and runs away. This automatically triggers the dog's hunting instinct, which could cause it to bite the cat.

What can happen?

Watch your four-legged friends closely. When the dog wags its tail amiably, and the cat invites the dog to romp around with play gestures, the spell is broken and the friendship sealed. This takes a while, because the cat does not know right away what the tail wagging means. It shows it somewhat differently: It gently bites the dog's tail, which the dog also must get used to.

When have they made friends?

The dog tries to be friendly, the cat misinterprets its gesture as a threat — and vice versa. This is the reason for many misunderstandings. In their life together the two must first learn the other's "foreign language."

Dog language — cat language

Beware, I am big and strong, approach me submissively, says the dog, when it raises

Raised tail

59

its tail. The cat, on the other hand, shows that it is in a friendly mood and wants to be petted.

Raised paws
I want your attention, play with me, the dog is trying to say, when it lifts its paw slightly (be nice to me, when it raises them). Beware when the cat lifts its paw, because it is preparing to take a swipe.

"Bowing"
I want to play with you, signals the dog, when it "bows" (presses its upper body to the floor and stretches its paws forward). This gesture means exactly the opposite with the cat: it shows that it wants to be left alone now.

Lying on the back
A dog presents its throat and belly to its opponent when it "gives up" and lies on its back. The cat assumes the supine position when it feels threatened, and in this way reveals its weapons — the sharp claws.

Staring
Cats stare at the cat sitting opposite, because it is customary among their kind to make contact in this way and through particular looks to signal if they have good intentions. Among dogs it is not customary to stare at others, because this is more likely to make the four-legged friend aggressive.

Can the dog and cat infect each other?
There are only a few diseases that can be transmitted from the dog to the cat and vice versa.

• Ear mites

Cats are rather insensitive to ear mites and for a long time exhibit hardly any symptoms when they are infected. They can infect the dog, however, which then exhibits severe symptoms of illness. With ear mites, the cat must always receive treatment too, or it will infect the dog again.

• Scabies

This condition can also be transmitted between dogs and cats and vice versa. Always treat both.

• Tapeworms, salmonella

Tapeworms, such as the pumpkinseed-like canine tapeworm, and certain bacteria, such as salmonella, can also be transmitted between the four-legged friends. The dog and cat must always be dewormed at the same time!

• Fleas

These parasites also jump from dog to cat and vice versa!

• Feline parvovirus

The cat cannot be infected with this virus by the dog, and vise versa.

• Keep dogs away from the litter box

Some dogs are "drawn" by litter boxes, the contents of which they eat. If you have a dog and notice that it has this bad habit, it is best to put the litter box in the bathroom.

Hammer a small nail into the door frame, and tie the nail to the door handle with a string. The crack of the door should be just wide enough for your cat, but not your dog, to get through.

If the dog is as small as the cat or smaller, put a board in front of the dog, so that the cat can jump over it, but the dog cannot.

Another possibility is to put the litter box in the bathtub. This is no problem for the cat, but a small dog cannot get in.

THE CHILD AND THE CAT

Anyone who had a cat as a child knows how much a pussycat can mean to a young person. Its manner of expression ranges from playful and cuddly to independent. Also, children can learn a great deal from a cat. For example, it can bring the understanding that each living creature also has a right to a life of its own, that they may not always impose themselves, and that despite this a close friendship can develop. Cats also learn to accept their playmate: Many cats develop a good sense of when a child is sadfor instance and needs intimacy.

Valuable playmate

Parents naturally must prepare their children for the cat. You should never "hand over" a cat, whether it is still very young or already somewhat older, to uninformed children. Children are often very loud, shrill, and sometimes rather rough in the demonstrations of their affection. Cats, however, hate noise and commotion.

Prepare children in advance

Therefore, you must explain to your children that they must wait for the affection of a cat and should observe it closely, so that they learn its language and how to react appropriately. Once the cat becomes frightened and neurotic, you will hardly be able to regain its trust again.

Affection is always returned

The cat will reward understanding and patience with affection and great tenderness. Cats always return the affection they receive, although they do so only when they want to. Cats are wonderful playmates as long as you respect their independence and give them time. This may sometimes be a difficult test for the children to face, but it is a good and important experience.

Watch the cat together

The parents together with the child should approach the kitten, particularly at first, and explain to the child what kind of mood the kitten is in. If it rolls over on its back boisterously or makes inviting jumps, it is ready to play. If it winds its way around your legs and purrs or rubs its head against them, then nothing stands in the way of petting it.

Handle with care

If, on the other hand, the cat goes away or hides, the child may, in no case, run after it, much less try to pull the cat out of its hiding place. Although cats usually put up more with children than adults — the children also must follow certain rules. Cats also do not like to be picked up unexpectedly, and react with great displeasure when you pull on their tail.

Explain and observe

Children have good powers of observation. If you give them an appropriate explanation, they will soon be able to gauge by the kitten's facial expression

Since 1952, Tropical Fish Hobbyist has been the source of accurate, up-to-the-minute, and fascinating information on every facet of the aquarium hobby. Join the many thousands of devoted readers worldwide who wouldn't miss a single issue.

Subscribe right now
so you don't miss a single copy!

SM 402

Reptile Hobbyist is the source for accurate, up-to-the-minute, practical information on *every* facet of the herpetological hobby. Join many thousands of devoted readers worldwide who wouldn't miss a single valuable issue.

Subscribe right now
so you don't miss a single copy!

and posture what mood the kitten is in at the moment.

Frequently you find cats in families with an only child. Cats are particularly popular with girls. One of the reasons for this, certainly, is that they are so cuddly.

Girls are especially fond of cats

Cat mothers carry their young by the scruff of the neck. Neither you nor your children should do this, especially not with adult cats. This hurts the animals or at least is unpleasant to them. Show your child the best way to carry the pussycat: With the left hand, hold the cat between the front legs under the chest and at the same time support the hind-quarters with the other hand. Then lift the cat and immediately bring it in to your body.

Carry the cat correctly

Tell your child never to lift the kitten by the shoulders, because this could dislocate its legs.

When the cat has been accustomed to being carried around (correctly) from the time it was a kitten, it will be fond of it. Cats like having a view from a height. They, of course, also like to sit in places from where they can enjoy the view. Nevertheless, never pick them up against their will.

Wonderful view

Cats are as sensitive over nearly their entire bodies as we humans are on the fingertips, because they have many nerve cells and are sensitive to touch every-

Many nerve cells

where. For this reason they are also quite responsive to petting. This is also the reason, however, why pussycats react so sensitively when you touch them inappropriately or roughly.

Addition to the family

When a change in the family is imminent, the cat is very conscious of it. For example, when a baby is on the way. The pussycat may then react as jealously as a child would to a new sibling. Therefore, you should consider a few things:

Cats are no danger

Some women want the cat out of the house as fast as possible when they are expecting a child, because they are afraid of the possibility of infection. In no case, however, give your housemate away for this reason. The danger of being infected by another person is far greater than the danger of being infected by a cat.

There are very few animal diseases that are communicable to human beings (see chapter "Danger of infection by the Cat"). Otherwise, there is no danger as long as the cat does not have a behavioral disorder and you do not neglect it, but rather accustom it to the baby.

Give it plenty of attention right away

During your pregnancy and following birth, give the cat just as much attention as before (not more, but not less either). The cat will not feel that its position is threatened by the new family member, but rather along with you accepts the baby as the center of attention. In no case should you shut it out of your life.

Include the cat in the reorganized family life, but the pussycat must also learn, with your help, what it is allowed to do with the baby. The cradle and crib must remain strictly taboo, as must the toys, pacifiers, and pieces of clothing. Only in your presence may the cat sniff at the baby, be near the baby carriage, or watch while you change a diaper.

Crib off limits

The cat may not touch small children without supervision either. They are fascinated by cats, because their appearance corresponds to the "child pattern": round head, big eyes, awkward movements. Furthermore, younger cats, in particular, are as playful as children. Children may not play with the animal alone until they are about four or five years old.

Supervise small children

Not until the child is about eight years old can he or she have sole responsibility for his or her pussycat. Before that the child should grow into this task, in that the parents gradually permit the child to brush the cat, to feed it, to give it water, to clean the litter box, and so forth.

Gradually transfer responsibility

If you have never had a cat and your children would like to have a pussycat as a playmate, select a fairly young, but adult cat, who is accustomed to children and is gentle and is not shy.

Which cat for your child?

WHAT THE CAT IS TRYING TO SAY

"Love song" What we often assume to be a "love song," when we hear a long drawn-out caterwauling at night, is in fact a threat that tomcats emit before a fight over "the one they worship."

If one of the rivals proves the stronger, the loser emits a very high-pitched screeching.

Purring Purring can mean various things. When it purrs, the cat usually is expressing its well-being, when it wants to be petted or while it is being petted. The louder and more intensely it purrs, the happier it feels.

When the cat greets its people, you can hear a soft purring.

If a tomcat is trying to "convince" a female cat, it tries to do so with a very long drawn-out "meow."

When a mother cat calls its kittens, it produces a soft, rounded purring, which in fact does sound something like "purr."

Cats also try to comfort themselves, such as when they are in great pain or are dying.

With a little kitten this can mean: "I feel lonely, where is my mother?" or "I am hungry." In any case, the kitten is saying that it is not satisfied and wants a change in its situation. **Meowing**

Cats emit a deep, hollow-sounding "wrau" when they are extremely afraid.

Curious cats tilt their ears forward and watch the object of their curiosity with big eyes and great interest. **Curious**

If caution is called for in a situation, the cat draws its body together and arches its back slightly. The tail is on the ground, and the ears are raised. **Cautious**

When you call your cat and it does not budge and demonstratively looks in another direction, it wants nothing to do with you at the moment. **No desire at the moment**

If the cat sits down in front of you, stretches its tail out on the floor in a relaxed manner, and watches you with interest, it wants to know what its owner has brought back, or whether you will show it something of interest. **What are you doing?**

If the cat holds its ears flat, if it holds its whiskers close to its head, if it twitches the tip of its tail and hisses softly, it is best to leave it alone. This is an advance warning that you should not come closer just now. **Leave me alone!**

If you continue to try to touch the cat, it will hiss more loudly, whip its tail to and fro, **Final warning** and make a defensive threat gesture with its paw as a final warning before it "strikes."

I am afraid

When the cat cowers on the floor with its tail drawn in under its belly and presses its hindquarters to the floor, it is afraid. If it also tilts its upper body to the side, presses it to the floor, and emits a gurgling meow, it is in a panicy fear.

I had better get out of here

If the pussycat fears an unpleasant encounter, it presses its hindquarters and tail to the floor, slinks away, and keeps an eye on the "unpleasant situation."

THE CAT AND VACATION

Whereas dogs always want to be near their owners and you therefore can and should take them along on vacation, in general cats do not like to travel. They like their home and a settled, quiet daily routine. The best solution is for the cat to stay home and be cared for in the familiar surroundings.

Cats do not like to travel

Ask relatives or friends to feed the cat, clean the litter box, and to spend a little time with it every day to keep it from feeling lonely. The entrusted person, however, should already be familiar to the cat beforehand. The person should practice caring for the cat at least once, so that everything goes smoothly. In this way the pussycat will also get used to the new person right away.

Relatives or friends take care of the cat

You can also leave the cat with relatives or friends. You should know the people, however, and they should not live in a house with a yard! If they do, there is the great danger that the cat could escape and try to return home. Bring the following items with you when you drop off the cat: sufficient food, sleeping basket, cushion or blanket, litter box, familiar toys, and always the veterinarian's address.

To relatives or friends

THE CAT AND VACATION

Preparation Buy enough food to last while you are gone, and leave money and the telephone number of your veterinarian for emergencies. Also, have a cat carrier ready.

Cat kennel Responsible kennels board only vaccinated, neutered, and healthy cats. These kennels naturally are crowded during vacation season. Therefore, make reservations as early as possible. You can obtain addresses from veterinarians, animal protection societies, or friends who own cats.

When there is no other choice... When you have absolutely no choice, and you have to bring your cat with you, it is still the best when you, for example, always go to the same vacation house. At a campground or in a motel, the cat would be under a great deal of stress, and there would be a substantial danger of it running away. It would have to be locked up at all times.

How to transport the cat? The drive in the car is already a horror for many cats. Therefore, you should prepare the animal for the trip ahead of time. It absolutely must travel in a lockable pet carrier (preferably of the cage type). Some cats, however, do not like to go in the carrier, because they usually associate it with the visit to the veterinarian. This is how you can reduce this mistrust:

• Put a towel on your cat's sleeping place for several days, so that it accepts the smell.

• Set out the pet carrier in the house, leave the door open, and put the towel inside. The cat will eye the carrier and finally, cautiously, go inside. Do not close the door at first, however, so that it can get out at any time.

• Close the door at first only for a short time, and open it right away, so that the cat sees that it can escape again.

• Increase the amount of time that the door is closed. When you open it, never take the cat out, but wait until it comes out on its own.

• Finally, carry the carrier around with the cat, so that it gets used to the swinging movement.

• Sit with your cat in the car, and let it explore its surroundings. (Keep the windows and doors closed, so that it does not escape!)

Acclimation to the car

• Start the engine, to get the animal used to the sound. Talk soothingly to it, and praise it if it is "good."

• Put the pussycat in the closed pet carrier, put it on the back seat (secure it with the seatbelts, so that it does not slide off the seat when you hit the breaks!), and drive a short distance.

On a longer trip, do not give the cat anything to eat before and during the drive, or give it only a very little, easily

The trip begins

digestible food if you know that your animal is not sensitive. Just before you leave, put the cat in the litter box one more time.

What you need

Bring along a plastic litter box with litter and a lid as well as drinking water. Do not forget the vaccination certificate when traveling abroad. Have the veterinarian prescribe medication against vomiting and diarrhea, and possibly eyedrops. Bring along the leash and harness as well as familiar toys and sleeping blanket or basket.

Stop frequently

On longer trips, stop occasionally. If you want to let the cat walk a little, make sure you use the harness and leash! The animal need only suddenly become frightened by a noise or a strange environment and it will be gone! Also, give it drinking water frequently. Do not wait for it to start panting with thirst, because the pussycat could go into shock. Naturally, do not leave the cat sitting in the car in the heat or cold!

THE CAT HAS DISAPPEARED

A shock, the cat is gone! Outdoor cats, in particular, are in danger of eventually not returning home. They can be run over, poisoned, or attacked by another animal. Therefore, cats should be brought inside the house at night at least, when the most can happen.

Search immediately

It also happens again and again that curious cats, during their explorations, fall into a shaft or hide in their own or a neighbor's basement, and are accidentally locked in. Do not immediately think the worst. Maybe the pussycat has hidden itself somewhere in the house. Nevertheless, you should start to search immediately.

If you have a house cat, first search through all corners, boxes, chests, closets, and drawers. Many pussycats have made themselves comfortable in an open closet, only to have the unsuspecting owner inadvertently lock it in, and then search desperately for his or her pet.

Locked in a cabinet

Search the stairwell from top to bottom, and ask the tenants whether the cat perhaps walked into another apartment.

In another apartment

Maybe the cat slipped in while your neighbor left the door open because of moving or renovations. Search your basement, which for the same reason may have been open for a while. At the same time, repeatedly call to the cat.

Fled out of fear
If your cat is permitted to go outside and you suspect that it is hiding there, you must search within a radius of about 300 to 500 yards. As mentioned previously, maybe it has hidden itself in a neighbor's basement or has fled into the nearest hiding place in panic, because, for example, it was chased by a dog or a human. In this case, it will not dare to emerge very quickly and may not come out when it hears voices.

Search in every corner
You must search with "the eyes of a cat." Think where you would hide if you were a cat. If other people help in the search, they should only be persons that the cat knows. It is best to cause as little commotion as possible. Only the owner should call to it; if the cat hears other voices, it could become even more panicky, especially if it is injured or terrified. Look behind and under every wood pile and bush, in every shed and corner. If the cat can fit its head through an opening, it can get its whole body through!

Ask the neighbors
Ask the neighbors for permission to look inside their garages, basements, and sheds, or at least have the neighbors themselves look. Also, ask them to notify you if they find your cat, because it

probably will not allow itself to be touched by strangers and may find an even better hiding place.

Within a radius of about 500 yards, post a notice on street corners, in stores, and at bus stops, and offer a small reward to anyone who finds the animal. Give an exact description of the cat and report any special features that might be present.

Lost-and-found notice

Search in the evening, when it is dark and quiet. Bring along the cat's favorite food. If the cat is accustomed, for example, to the rattling of the dry-food box or other "food sounds," then you can lure the animal in this manner. Continually repeat its name softly and then wait a few minutes before you slowly move on. If you are accompanied by someone, this person absolutely must keep quiet.

Preferably in late evening

When the cat sees you while you are searching for it, it can happen that the animal will not call out or come because it thinks that you see it, too.

The cat sees, but is not seen

If you do not live far from a cemetery, it is worthwhile to search there. Many cats like to stay in such a place because it is quiet.

Popular: cemetery

Inquire at the nearest animal shelter and surrounding shelters. Stray cats are often reported or brought there. Maybe your pussycat is already waiting for you.

Inquire at the animal shelter

You absolutely must, however, go there in person at least once. Telephone conversations are often misunderstood. Sometimes, not even the owner is sure if he is looking at his animal, because as a result of terrible experiences the cat has changed its behavior, has become emaciated or been injured, and therefore looks different.

Call the vet

Call all the veterinarians in the vicinity. Maybe someone has brought the possibly injured or sick animal in for treatment!

Nothing escapes the mailman's notice

Above all, if you live in the country, explain to the mailman that you are looking for your cat. The mailman usually gets on the road very early and may have heard of a stray, or found cat in the neighborhood. He or she may even have seen the animal.

Call the police

Call the police. If the cat was run over, they may know about it at the police station.

Do not give up

Do not abandon the search. Some people who find a cat, or are adopted by it, do not report this for weeks.

Give the "all clear signal"

If you have found your pet, in your joy do not forget to give the "all clear signal" in all the places, and to all the people, you notified about the cat's disappearance. Also, do not forget to take down all lost-and-found notices.

Nameplate under the skin

With a so-called microchip, a "nameplate" under the skin, you can have the cat marked at the veterinarian. These animals are then registered in a file. This also makes it easier for the finder of a cat to return it to its rightful owner. Another advantage: Cats marked in this way are not as suitable for experimental purposes, because they are clearly identifiable.

It happens time and again that cats jump out of the car shortly after an accident, run away, and hide somewhere. Owners are often successful when they stay a fairly long time near the scene of the accident, or return in the evening for a number of days and put out food and an object that smells of the cat and wait in the car. Call out the cat's name repeatedly!

Automobile accident

Cats should be transported in the car in standard cat carriers. The carriers can be closed securely and are not easily damaged, so that they also offer the cat protection. Sometimes the cat itself can even open the carriers.

Cat carriers are the safest

When someone dies or is seriously ill and must go into the hospital, many cats have starved wretchedly because they have hidden somewhere in the home out of fear of the strange people, and the home was sealed.

Owner deceased, is the cat locked in?

When you know that within your circle of relatives or acquaintances a deceased or ill person had a cat, make sure that the cat is found and cared for. It is best to set up a special cat trap (which has nothing in common with the cruel forms of animal traps) with food and water to lure the cat to you and capture it.

A SECOND CAT ARRIVES

It is not always easy with a new companion If you work, a cat is ideal. Unlike a dog, you can leave it alone all day. Nevertheless, cats sometimes suffer from boredom, particularly when the home does not offer sufficient opportunity to play and explore. A second animal is the best solution. If you have already owned your first cat for a fairly long time, however, sometimes it is not all that easy for it to accept a new one. Curiously, cats often adjust more readily to a dog (as long as they have not had bad experiences with them) than to another cat, because often they are more jealous of others of their own kind.

Different sexes In 80 to 90 percent of the cases, the cats adjust successfully if you take an animal of the opposite sex that is of approximately the same age. (Naturally, both must be neutered!)

Do not put a very young cat with an old one Many believe that they are doing their older cat a big favor by acquiring a very young kitten, because it will trigger the maternal instinct. This happens only rarely. Your mature, quiet cat probably will not like it much when an energentic kitten plays with its tail and constantly jumps around it. If you happen to find a kitten, however, you should try it anyway before you try to find another home for it.

When the new cat arrives in the home, never pet one of the two animals, much less pick one up! If you pick up the new pussycat and thereby carry its scent, it can happen that your own, otherwise peaceful cat, will reject you or even scratch you. How the business eventually turns out depends for the most part on your behavior.

Do not touch either cat

It is best for the cats to become acquainted without your intervention. Hissing is a greeting ceremony, in which the animals, so to speak, measure their strength. If they do not attack each other, you should not intervene.

Do not intervene

Your cat or cats will detect and see by your behavior precisely whether you support them. Then the pussycats will fight the newcomer with, so to speak, your support. If, however, you pay attention to the new cat, the others will be jealous. Therefore, it is important that you behave neutrally and do not interfere. This is the best way to proceed:

Stay neutral

• Call your cat or cats into a room. The room should not be too small, and if possible should not have any hiding places.

Neutral behavior

• Then bring in the newcomer (keeping them several meters apart), and at the same time talk soothingly to all the animals.

• Now leave the task of becoming acquainted to the animals, but remain nearby. Things will probably get heated now, with hissing and chasing. Only rarely does serious fighting occur, in which you will have to intervene after all.

• You should set up the feeding place in one room, but keep the dishes a safe distance apart. It is important that the animals always eat together in the same room.

• After some time (two, three weeks), although the new cat usually will not be well liked, it will at least be left in peace. Stay neutral!

Friendship grows

• Finally the hatchet will be buried, and the animals will begin to examine and sniff each other. Now you should pet both/all animals together and talk to them. In this way the cats will understand that you are fond of them all, and the danger of jealousy will be averted.

• Gradually move the food dishes closer and closer together.

• If you now notice that the cats have accepted each other, you can pick up your old-established cat, sit near the newcomer, and let them sniff each other. Then do the reverse. Avoid putting the cats face to face, however, because this could make them feel threatened again. They can also sniff at other parts of each other's bodies.

• If you notice that one of the cats does not feel comfortable with this approach, then immediately stop and try it again later. An ideal way to get the cats acquainted is to play with them.

• Eventually the cats will get along well, play with each other, and wrestle. Have patience, however, because it sometimes takes many weeks to get to this point.

BODY CARE

Coat care   Although cats spend a large part of the day grooming themselves thoroughly, they also need the supplemental help of the owner to take care of the coat. Brushing and combing not only removes dead hair and flakes of dandruff, it also stimulates the circulation, and improves muscle tone. A shiny, soft coat is a sign of the cat's health and vitality. The type and frequency of coat care depends on whether you have a long-haired or short-haired cat.

The care of the long-haired cat   Long-haired cats must be combed and brushed daily, to prevent the formation of knots and matted fur. It is best to take 15 to 30 minutes, twice a day, for the care of your four-legged friend. For this purpose, you need a coarse-toothed and a fine-toothed metal comb as well as a wire brush with curved metal bristles. A natural-hair brush is also suitable. With the coarse-toothed comb, first remove the knots and comb out the hair mats. Only when the coarse-toothed comb glides through the coat effortlessly can you switch to the brush. Use the brush to remove the dead hair. To achieve a particularly full coat, you can dust the cat with talcum powder. You must brush the powder out thoroughly, however, after a short time. After brushing, groom the hair in the neck and nape region into an attractive ruff with the fine-toothed comb. Brush the shorter hair on the cat's face carefully with a toothbrush. Finally, loosen up the coat again with the coarse-toothed comb.

First, separate stubborn knots in the coat with the fingers into small parts and then untangle them with the sharp handle of a comb.

Knots of hair

Long-haired cats, whose owners do not spend enough time caring for the coat, sometimes have matted hair over their whole body, giving the impression that the cat is inside a shell. With such extensive matting, air can no longer reach the skin. Eczema and itching result under the shell of fur. Only the veterinarian can help here. He removes the matted hair with curved scissors and the shearing machine. This is usually possible only under anesthesia, because if the animal were to struggle, it could easily suffer deep cuts in the skin. Only when the matted shell is removed can the veterinarian treat the acute eczema.

Extensive hair mats

Pull the matted hair away from the skin with a comb, and then cut it off above the comb. If you neglect to do this, the hair could become so matted with feces that the anus could be blocked, and the animal could no longer defecate.

Matted hair in the anal region

To care for the coat of your short-haired cat, you only need to plan on 30 minutes

The care of the

short-haired cat

once a week. First, comb the cat from head to tail with a fine-toothed comb. Then brush again from head to tail with a nubbly rubber brush. Brush first with the grain of the hair, then carefully against the grain, and finally once more with the grain. The last thing you do is wipe with the grain over the coat with a damp chamois cloth or bath towel. This removes the remaining dust, and gives the coat a sheen.

When the winter coat is shed

When shedding occurs, with short-haired cats run your hand through the coat before combing and brushing it. And make sure you do it against the grain! In this way you loosen the dead hair and bring it to the surface. Finally, you can brush it out thoroughly. This is important, because dead hair can cause intense itching.

May you bathe cats?

Of course, you may bathe cats! How often you will have to bathe your cat depends on whether you own a normal house cat or a long-haired pedigreed cat. House cats very rarely need a bath, unless, for example, they are infested with parasites. Long-haired cats, on the other hand, need to bathe considerably more frequently. Cats whose coats quickly becomes oily must be bathed more frequently. Do not, however, bathe the cat more often than once a month.

What is the right way to bathe a

The kitchen or bathroom sink is the right size for bathing a cat. To keep the cat from slipping, place a non-slip rubber mat on the bottom of the sink. The water temperature should correspond to the cat's body temperature. Thus, it should be about 98° Fahrenheit. The bath water may reach no higher than the belly of the standing cat. Before you put the animal in the water, put some eye ointment in both eyes. This will prevent shampoo from stinging the eyes. To keep water from getting in the ears, block the ear canals with balls of cotton wool. Then put the cat in the water, and lather it thoroughly with special cat or baby shampoo. While you are doing this, hold your pet tightly by the front paws. Rinse the shampoo out thoroughly, because soapy residue could irritate the skin.

cat?

After you finish the bath, take the cat out of the sink, and wrap it in a large, pre-warmed hand towel. Now you can wash the face with a washcloth dipped in warm water. Until the cat is completely dry, it must stay in a warm place.

Must you dry the cat?

If you want to use a hair dryer to dry the coat, you should accustom the cat to it before the first bath. In any case, use the hair dryer's lowest setting, and make sure that you do not singe the fur.

Can you use a hair dryer?

To comb the cat, put the cat on your lap. First, comb carefully with the coarse-toothed comb — especially on the belly and between the legs. After that, comb again with the fine-toothed comb.

Combing after the bath

With very young kittens, the danger of catching cold is of course much greater

May you bathe

young kittens? than with adult cats. Kittens that are younger than 12 weeks should not be bathed. If necessary, you can bathe kittens that are older than 12 weeks and have already had their basic immunizations. Dry the kitten particularly thoroughly, and make sure that it is not exposed to draft.

How do you bathe an uncooperative cat? If your cat offers strong resistance to the bath, put it in a linen sack with only the head sticking out. Pour the shampoo in the sack and then submerge the cat and the sack in the water. Massage the animal through the sack, so that lather forms. In this way you will clean the cat.

Dry shampoos With especially uncooperative cats, it is advisable to use a dry shampoo. Work it into the coat thoroughly against the grain. Let it take effect for a short time, and then brush the cat thoroughly. You can obtain dry shampoos from various manufacturers on the market.

Do cats need "claw care"? Cats that are allowed to go outside do not need any claw care at all, because the claws of outdoor cats are automatically worn down and sharpened. With house cats that never go outside, however, you should examine the claws occasionally, because the claws can grow into the pads if they are too long. This condition can be very painful and can lead to an abscess. Furthermore, overly long claws readily get caught in carpets, curtains, and upholstered furniture. This can lead to a painful torn nail.

If possible, you should leave this task to an expert — a breeder or veterinarian — because the claws should only be trimmed with special clippers. The clippers fit around the round shape of the cat claw, do not crush the nail, and cut them diagonally from the front, without hurting the cat. You should not use nail clippers for humans, because they are designed for the flat human nail shape.

Is it difficult to trim the claws?

If you want to clip the claws yourself, put your cat in your lap. Then press with one hand on the pad of the foot, so that the claws come out. Then clip off only the thin, sharp tip of the claw with the cat clippers (available in pet stores). In no case may you clip higher up on the thicker part of the claw, because there is the danger of cutting into the quick. This would cause serious bleeding, and the pain would frighten the cat.

This is how to clip the claws

Yes, it is very important! The story is the same here as well: an ounce of prevention is better than a pound of cure. Through strict oral hygiene, the cat, too, can retain sparkling white, healthy teeth for many years.

Is tooth care important?

Only with very patient cats is it possible to clean the teeth with a child's toothbrush and toothpaste for dogs. The vast majority of cats do not tolerate this. It is easier if you wrap an index finger with a cloth, apply a little baking soda and water paste to it, and carefully clean the teeth and gums with it.

Cleaning the teeth

May you use lemon juice?

Never use lemon juice to clean the teeth, because the acid attacks the tooth enamel and makes it rough.

Must you remove tartar?

Yes, absolutely! Tartar is dangerous for the teeth. It is a first-class carrier of bacteria and causes bad breath, cavities, and gingivitis. It also leads to the loosening and loss of the teeth. Furthermore, it can cause painful inflammation of the gums. The gums can get so painful that the animal finally refuses to eat at all. Therefore, the tartar absolutely must be removed at least once a year. This is a routine procedure for the veterinarian. The cat is given a mild anesthetic, and the procedure is completed with ultrasound, without damaging the tooth enamel.

Eye care

The care of the eyes with short-haired cats is limited to wiping the eye with a damp linen cloth. Always wipe from the outside in; that is, from the outside corner of the eye in toward the nose. This procedure also removes light encrustations in the corner of the eye. Do not use a wad of cotton wool or a paper towel to clean the eye, because the cat could get fibers in its eyes.

Tear stains with long-haired cats

Long-haired cats are susceptible to plugging of the tear ducts. When they are plugged, the tears will not be able to flow out of the tear ducts. Instead, they run down along the nose and produce ugly, dark stripes on the face.

Removing tear

Dip a linen cloth in a weak saltwater solution and use it to wash off the stains, or buy a special commercial tear-stain cleaner at the pet store or from the veterinarian.

stains

Important: Never poke around in the ear canal with a cotton swab, because a healthy cat's ear cleans itself, and an infected ear requires veterinary treatment. Clean only the inside of the external ear with a cloth dunked in water or mineral oil. If too much hair is growing in the ear opening so that the ear canal no longer receives sufficient ventilation, you must pluck the hairs.

Be careful with the ears!

DIET

The cat is what it eats!
The first commandment in cat nutrition is: the cat is no garbage disposal. Kitchen and table scraps are in no way suitable for the cat's diet. Only a properly fed cat can be a healthy cat.

Human food is unsuitable
Human food contains too much fat, too many carbohydrates, and too little protein for the cat. Furthermore, leftovers are usually too highly seasoned.

Is the cat a pure carnivore?
This misconception is widespread. Cats fed exclusively meat do get sick. We can trace this back to their descent from wild cats. Wild cats ate not only the muscle meat of the prey animals, they also ate the stomach and intestines with the pre-digested vegetable matter they contained. In this way, they also took up carbohydrates and fats. The wild cats also ate bones, ligaments, tendons, and blood, and in this way met their mineral requirement.

Vegetarian diet?
No! Feeding a cat a vegetarian diet would be cruel, because cats are predators and need animal protein to stay healthy.

You can nourish your cat optimally with commercial food alone, because it contains, besides meat, also vegetable nutrients in a digestible form.

About commercial food

Canned food contains the basic nutrients— protein, carbohydrate, and fat in the proper proportions. It also contains all essential vitamins and minerals in sufficient quantity.

Canned food

Premium dry food also contain the nutrients cats need and their crunchy texture helps remove plaque on teeth. However, you should avoid feeding dry food exclusively, because very few cats will drink the extra amount of water they require to balance out the large amount of dry food. Calculus and stones in the urinary tract could be the result. Your veterinarian is your best source for advice in this area.

Dry food

No, dog food is not suitable for cats! Cats require much more protein than dogs (approximately twice as much) and require the essential amino acid taurine as a dietary supplement. Commercial food for cats contains sufficient amounts of taurine. Commercial food for dogs, on the other hand, contains no taurine at all, because dogs do not require it for their metabolism.

Is dog food suitable for cats?

Complete taurine deficiency in the cat's diet causes severe damage. After only a short time, the four-legged friend becomes totally blind, and the heart muscle suffers damage.

What about taurine deficiency?

Do not feed raw meat!	Cats should not be fed raw meat, to rule out the danger of infection with salmonella (chicken!), and other disease-causing organisms.
May cats eat fruit?	Although fruit is not essential for cats, if your cat shows an appetite for fruits you can safely satisfy this need. All kinds of fruit are suitable.
Can fruit pits harm the cat?	Because the cat does not have an appendix on the caecum, you need not fear smaller stones, such as cherry stones. Prune, apricot, and plum pits, however, can cause intestinal obstruction, because they cling to the intestinal wall. Furthermore, these pits contain small amounts of hydrocyanic acid, which could make the cat sick.
What about eggs?	Cooked eggs are a source of easy-to-digest protein, but never feed raw eggs! First, there is the danger of a salmonella infection, and, second, raw protein destroys the B vitamins and biotin in the diet.
Bones?	Bones are strictly forbidden.
Does the cat need drinking water regularly?	The cat must have water available to it around the clock. Always put the water dish in the same place, which must be easily accessible to the cat. Also, make sure that the dish is always filled with fresh water.
May cats drink	Whole milk is unsuitable as a drink for adult cats. They cannot digest the lac-

tose it contains, because they lack the necessary enzyme. The result of drinking milk is often severe diarrhea.

milk?

Milk products such as mild cheese or yogurt can be valuable supplements to the diet. They are well tolerated and digested by cats.

Are milk products allowed?

With cats that drink very little, you can increase the fluid intake by offering them a clear, defatted beef broth. Most cats are very fond of this soup.

Beef broth

Do not throw away the meat water that results from thawing frozen meat. Dilute it with some warm water and give it to your cat to drink. Even cats that normally drink almost nothing cannot resist it.

Meat water

Onions break down the red blood corpuscles in cats. The animals become apathetic and weak and the conjunctiva and mucous membranes turn a bluish color. So, make sure that you do not leave any leftover onion soup or other onion dish standing around, which the cat could "steal."

Onions

Cats must always have the opportunity to nibble on greens, such as cat grass. When they groom their coat they swallow a great deal of hair. If they do not eat grass, the hair gathers into large hair balls, which can cause constipation. If the cat has the opportunity to take in sufficient greens, however, the plant fi-

Greens

bers combine with the hairs, and the cat can readily cough or vomit them up.

Which greens are suitable?
You can buy cat grass in pet stores. Also, you can simply give your cat a pot of chives or sow a small meadow in a shallow dish. All tough-bladed grasses and all kinds of grains are suitable.

Leftovers in the food dish
Never leave leftover food in the dish, because it could turn sour, become permeated with bacteria, or be colonized by fly maggots. The cat could get sick with severe food poisoning. If your cat regularly leaves part of the food in the dish, then simply reduce the next ration by the leftover amount. Wash out the food dish with hot water after every meal, but do not use cleaning agents.

The temperature of the food
Regardless of whether you prepare the food yourself or use commercial food, it must never be too cold or too hot. Never give foods directly from the refrigerator, much less from the freezer! Warm the food to room temperature—this corresponds to the temperature of freshly killed prey animals. The microwave is very practical for warming the food.

Where should you put the food dish?
Because cats are very sensitive to noise, harsh light, and commotion, you should put the food dish in a quiet, secluded corner of the home. Pick out a suitable place from the start, which you can use throughout the cat's life.

How often
Feed adult cats—cats older than nine

months old—two to three times a day.

Feed at the same times every day. The cat soon gets used to the schedule, and then goes to the feeding place at the usual times. In this way, even cats that are allowed to go outside come home regularly.

How much your pussycat should and may eat cannot be answered with precise amounts. You must determine for yourself the amount of food your cat needs to stay healthy and trim. As with humans, there are cats with active and inactive metabolisms. A very active cat, of course, also needs more food than a lazy, inactive cat. To prevent obesity, you should weigh your four-legged friend regularly and keep a weight chart. If the cat has clearly gained weight, you must reduce the amount of food immediately.

How much may the cat eat?

Depending on their size, cats have an average energy requirement of 200 to 350 calories a day.

With pedigreed cats there is a prescribed ideal weight. It is best to ask about it when you buy the cat. Deviations above and below the ideal weight should not exceed ten percent.

Ideal weight for pedigreed cats

With normal house cats you must determine the ideal weight yourself by feeling the ribs and backbone from time to time. With a cat of normal weight, you must be

Ideal weight for house cats

able to feel the ribs and backbone easily through the skin. Generally, the average weight of a female house cat is five and a half to eight pounds, and the average weight of a tomcat is six and a half to ten pounds.

What should you do about loss of appetite?

Because problems with the teeth and gums very often are the reason for a loss of appetite in cats, you should have this cleared up immediately by the veterinarian. The veterinarian can also rule out other illnesses at the same time. If the cat is healthy, a loss of appetite is no cause for concern, because cats are often capricious and finicky about food. Provide a little more variety in the menu. If even this does not help, then go ahead and let the cat go hungry for a few days.

What are the causes of obesity?

The causes of obesity are overfeeding, improper diet (too much fat and too many carbohydrates), too many "between-meal snacks," and too little exercise.

What are the consequences of obesity?

Overweight cats are prone to heart and circulatory disorders, diabetes, and damage to the locomatory apparatus, which simply cannot handle the excess weight.

What can you do about obesity?

The simplest solution would be to reduce the normal food by a third until the ideal weight is attained. Because most obese cats, however, will react to the reduced amount of food with vigorous begging, a reduced-calorie diet is preferable, because you can feed this in the accustomed amount.

Commercial, reduced-calorie dietetic food is available from your veterinarian. With it the cat can lose weight without having to go hungry. The dietetic food can, of course, only work if it is fed exclusively. It is enriched with all essential vitamins and minerals, so that the cat will not develop deficiency symptoms even with long-term use. The only other thing the obese four-legged friend gets is fresh drinking water.

Weight loss with commercial dietetic food

No, this is just as invalid for the old cat as for the old human being. The old cat should even be thinner than a young cat, because the energy requirement decreases in old age.

May an old cat be more obese?

Diabetes occurs frequently in older, obese animals. Your veterinarian has special dietetic food for diabetic cats. It is particularly high in fiber and contains little fat and few carbohydrates. The high fiber content lowers the blood-sugar level after eating.

Diabetes

As is true of human beings, cats can also develop food allergies. These can be expressed in three ways: as gastro-enteritis with vomiting, diarrhea or both; as itchy dermatitis; or as a combination of gastro-enteritis and skin disorders.

Food allergies

You have the choice of preparing allergy-free food yourself for your pet every day or buying allergy-free commercial food from your veterinarian.

Allergies?

Nutrition of the kitten

At about eight weeks of age, kittens are weaned from the mother and usually go to their new owner. Now the important thing is for you to give the little kittens a healthy, balanced diet. Kittens need food that is richer in protein and minerals than do adult cats. The so-called canned kitten foods are well suited, because their mineral content covers the higher requirement during the growth phase.

How often must you feed kittens?

Up to an age of twelve weeks, kittens need five meals a day. Then, up to an age of five months, they need four meals. Starting at six months of age, you can acclimate the kitten to only two meals a day.

It makes sense to feed commercial kitten food up to the age of nine months.

Nutrition of the old cat

The sense of taste and smell deteriorate with age, so many older cats eat less, and there is the danger that they will not take in enough essential nutrients. Moreover, the old cat has special dietary needs. It needs, for example, particularly large amounts of vitamin A, B1, B2, B6, B12, and vitamin E. On the other hand, its energy requirement is reduced and it also needs less protein. Commercial foods formulated specifically for older cats are available. Feed these in small portions several times a day.

Old cats are susceptible

Old cats are prone to constipation, which frequently produces painful symptoms. The stool becomes hard and dry, and the animals have pain and cry out when they defecate. To make the stool softer, you should mix in two teaspoons of bran or melted butter to each meal.

to constipation

FIRST AID

Bee and wasp stings Stings to the tongue or in the throat are dangerous because they can become very swollen. There is the danger of suffocation! Put an ice cube in the mouth and bring the cat to the veterinarian as soon as possible! Stings to the paws cause swelling and itching. A cold, wet compress provides relief.

Allergic shock Some cats react to insect stings by going into allergic shock. Circulatory collapse, shallow breathing, and general weakness are the result. The legs feel cold and the mucous membranes are pale or blue in color. Shock is always a life-threatening condition. Wrap the cat immediately in warm blankets or aluminum foil to keep it from losing too much heat, and take it to the veterinarian immediately!

Tick bite Cover an attached tick with mineral oil or Vaseline and pull it off with a sharp twist. You can also dab the tick with concentrated alcohol and twist the parasite in a circle until it falls off.

Heat stroke The symptoms of heat stroke are rapid panting, shivering, seizures, and loss of consciousness. Bring the animal immediately into the shade or a cool room (basement!), spray it with cold water, and wrap the four-legged friend in cold, wet towels. Take the cat to the veterinarian without delay.

It is necessary to stop the bleeding immediately; press a compress firmly on the bleeding wound. Do not clean the wound. Instead, take the cat to the veterinarian immediately. The veterinarian will dress the wound correctly and treat the loss of blood and circulatory shock.

Profusely bleeding cuts

You may clean these yourself. First, remove the matted hair with blunt scissors, and then disinfect the wound. In the following days, bathe the wound several times a day with sage or mallow tea.

Superficial abrasions

These must be wrapped in layers from below, until no more blood seeps through. Practical for this purpose are adhesive bandages.

Bleeding paws

Bites often look harmless, but are always insidious! The canines of the rival tomcat tear deep "pockets" in the tissue under the skin. Because of the rapid growth of bacteria, abscesses often form. Therefore, clean bites thoroughly and have the veterinarian treat the cat with antibiotics within six hours.

Bites

Fill the crack with wax, so that it does not tear further. This will save the claw. The the cat to the veterinarian immediately.

Split or torn claws

Seizures   Such attacks usually look more serious than they are. They usually begin with abnormal behavior. The cat grinds its teeth noisily, makes chewing movements, produces foam from the mouth, twitches its legs, defecates and urinates, and finally loses consciousness. Determine if the cat is lying in a safe place. If it is, leave it where it is and cover it with a blanket to keep it warm. Then darken the room and turn off all sources of noise, such as radios, televisions, and household appliances. Never try to administer medications or liquids to the animal during the attack. The seizures usually stop in a few minutes. Then place the four-legged friend on a blanket and bring it to the veterinarian. An accurate description of the attack will make the veterinarian's diagnosis and therapy easier.

Poisoning   Cats can be poisoned in two ways: Either the coat is contaminated with poisonous substances, and the cat licks the poison off while grooming, or it eats poisoned prey animals. Symptoms include bleeding from the body cavities, vomiting, diarrhea, seizures, and loss of consciousness. Wash the cat with soap or shampoo to remove any remnants of poison from the coat, and give the animal charcoal tablets to neutralize at least some of the poison. Then see the veterinarian as soon as possible!

Vomiting   Do not feed the cat for a day. Give only mallow tea to drink. If the vomiting persists, you must take the cat to the veterinarian.

Diarrhea

Withhold food for a day and offer only chamomile tea or weak black tea to drink. Because of the danger of dehydration, bring the cat to the veterinarian as soon as possible.

Eye discharge

Clean the eye with cotton wool soaked in chamomile tea in the direction of the nose.

Foreign body in the eye

You may remove a foreign body from the eye if you can remove it easily. If this is not possible, put a wad of cotton wool soaked in cold chamomile tea on the eye, and bring the cat to the veterinarian immediately.

Foreign bodies in the nose

Never try to remove the foreign body yourself! Instead, as first aid, apply an ice-cold compress to the nose, to reduce bleeding. Then take the cat to the veterinarian immediately.

Earache

If the cat shakes its head constantly and scratches at its ears, it has an earache or infection, and you may spray an ear-cleaning agent into the ear. The veterinarian must do anything else.

Swallowing of small objects

If the cat has swallowed a small foreign body, give fiber-rich, bulky foods (sauerkraut, mashed potatoes) as a first aid measure. These will encase the foreign body and carry it along the digestive tract.

Sprains, bruises,

Wet the coat of the affected part of the body with cold water. In this way you achieve the

and swelling

effect of a cold compress, which prevents further swelling and relieves the pain.

Traffic accidents

After a traffic accident, you must always suspect the presence of internal injuries! Therefore, always handle an injured or unconscious cat very cautiously until you can get it to the veterinarian. To move the cat, pull a blanket under it, and carry the cat as if in a hammock. Never elevate the head of the injured cat, because there is the danger that saliva, blood, or vomit could get into the windpipe and then into the lungs. Trying to administer medications or water is also out of the question. Only cover the cat to keep it from becoming hypothermic. If necessary, you can administer heart massage and artificial respiration as first aid.

Heart massage

If you do not feel a pulse, massage the heart region vigorously, but carefully, because the ribs of the cat break easily.

Mouth-to-mouth resuscitation

First, wipe sticky blood or dirt from the nostrils to free the air passage. Then place your lips over the cat's nostrils and blow in air for three seconds. Then pause for two seconds. Repeat this procedure until the cat starts to breathe on its own.

Artificial respiration

Place the palms of your hands on the thorax above the ribcage, and then compress the thorax to force air into the lungs. Release the pressure, so that the thorax can expand again and the lungs can fill with air. Repeat the whole procedure at five second intervals.

Never try doing this with turpentine, gasoline, or other caustic chemicals. They could cause severe irritation of the skin. You can remove tar and grease effectively with vegetable oil, and then bathe the cat. As an exception, add a mild dishwashing liquid to the bath. The best way to remove paint is by carefully cutting out the matted hair.

To remove paint, tar, and motor oil

Snake bites most often occur on the cat's head or paws. You will be able to see the two closely spaced punctures of the fangs. Important: Calm the cat down and immobolize it, because otherwise the toxin will spread through the body even faster. If the snake bite is on the paw, you should apply a tourniquet above the bite, to keep the toxin from spreading fast. You can use a belt or shoelace as a tourniquet. Make sure that the tourniquet is not too tight, because although the circulation must be reduced, it must not be cut off completely (danger of gangrene of the paw). Wrap the cat in a blanket and take it as quickly as possible to the veterinarian.

Snake bite

If these are only superficial, that is, the surface of the skin at the affected site is red and painful, but not broken, run cold water over it for a few minutes. Then apply a cold compress. If the burn or scald has also damaged deeper layers of skin, however, only cover the wound with a clean cloth, and bring the cat immediately to the veterinarian.

Burns and scalds

FIRST AID

Electric shock　　This happens frequently with kittens that chew through electric cables. After an electric shock, cats usually lie unconscious on their side, suffer burns, lose urine and feces, and sometimes also experience cardiac arrest. Never touch the animal as long as it is still in contact with the source of current. Turn off the current immediately! Then bring the cat to the veterinarian immediately.

Hypothermia　　Short-haired, young, and injured cats are particularly susceptible to hypothermia. Animals suffering from hypothermia feel cold, shiver, have strongly dilated pupils, and a below-normal body temperature. Warm the cat slowly by wrapping it in a warm blanket. Put a hot-water bottle on the outside of the blanket — not directly on its coat! Cats suffering from hypothermia burn easily, because the skin has very poor circulation. Finally, you can give the cat a warm bath. Make sure that its head always stays above water.

Frostbite　　When cats roam around in sub-zero temperatures, it can happen that they will come home with frostbite. Usually the tips of the ears and tail are affected, sometimes the paws as well. The frostbitten areas feel dry and leathery. Do not make the mistake of rubbing the frozen body part with snow or rough material, because this would only injure the frozen tissue. The right way to do it is to wrap the cat in a blanket and to thaw the affected body parts with the warmth of your hands.

This happens most frequently following a fall into a swimming pool, because the cat cannot climb the ladder to get out and must swim till exhaustion. After rescuing the four-legged friend from the water, pull its tongue out, and make sure that the water can run out by holding the cat by the hind legs and letting it hang head down. You can hold the cat by the hind legs and whirl it in a circle, so that the centrifugal force hurls the water out of the air passages. When the air passages are free, begin with artificial respiration. Only when the cat breathes independently again may you dry it off and wrap it in a warm blanket. In the following days, the cat should be kept under veterinary supervision.

Drowning

MEDICAL CARE

Taking the temp-erature

When you want to take your cat's temperature, a second person should hold the cat by the scruff of the neck. Then you should lubricate the thermometer and lift the tail with one hand, and with the other hand insert the thermometer deep into the anus. Never let go of the thermometer as long as it is sticking in the cat's anus.

It is best to tie a string tightly around the indented end of the thermometer, so that you can withdraw it quickly should the cat get restless.

Depending on the cat's age, the normal temperature is 99 to 101° Fahrenheit.

Kittens and pregnant cats have a higher temperature than fully grown animals and those that are not pregnant.

Never measure the temperature immediately after the cat eats or after physical exertion, because the temperature rises slightly at these times.

Taking the pulse

Because many laypersons have a hard time taking their cat's pulse by pressing on the big femoral artery on the inside of the thigh, you can count the heartbeats instead. For this purpose, place one hand on the cat's chest directly below the left elbow joint. Move your hand around until you feel the heartbeat. Then count the number of beats in 20 seconds and multiply the result by three.

An example: You have counted 40 beats in the 20 seconds. This means that the cat in question has a pulse rate of 120 beats per minute. The normal pulse rate of cats is 108 to 132 beats per minute.

A healthy cat takes 20 to 30 breaths per minute. Watch the thorax and count how often it rises in 20 seconds. Multiply the result by three. It would be wrong to count both the rise and fall of the thorax.

Counting breaths per minute

Because most veterinary clinics are equipped with an animal scale, you should make sure on each visit to the veterinarian that your cat is weighed and the result recorded. The normal weight of a house cat is five to ten pounds.

Weighing

Even the hardiest cat is defenseless against viral diseases. Only vaccination can protect your cats from them.

Vaccination

The earliest time for the initial feline-distemper vaccination is at an age of nine weeks. Two vaccinations are given within a period of three weeks. The second vaccination must never be forgotten, because it is necessary to provide the full protection provided by the vaccine. After

Feline distemper vaccination

that only an annual booster shot is required.

Vaccination against upper respiratory infections

Upper respiratory infections are dangerous viral diseases of the upper air passages and are very unpleasant for the cat. An annual vaccination protects your pet against them. In the first year of immunization, this vaccination also must be repeated after three weeks. The vaccine for upper respiratory infections is also available as a combination vaccine with the feline distemper vaccine.

Feline leukemia vaccination

Definitely have your cat vaccinated against this widespread disease that weakens the immune system. The basic immunization consists of two injections at a two- to four-week interval. An annual booster shot is required.

FIP vaccination

Feline infectious peritonitis (FIP) is a dreaded viral disease of cats. The most conspicuous symptom to the cat's owner is the abdomen, which exhibits a pear-shaped swelling due to the accumulation of fluids. There is now a vaccine against this disease as well. What is unusual about the FIP vaccination is that the vaccine is not administered in the form of an injection, but is administered uniformly into both nostrils in the same way as nose drops by the veterinarian. Two basic immunizations at an interval of four to six weeks, and an annual booster shot, offer good protection. All healthy cats can be vaccinated at sixteen weeks of age.

Only cats that are allowed to go outside must be vaccinated against rabies. Cats that always stay indoors do not need this vaccination. The first rabies vaccination is possible at the cat's third month of life. A second vaccination after four weeks is necessary to ensure full immunity. After that, a booster shot is required once a year.

Rabies vacci- nation

Even if the cat exhibits no symptoms of a worm infestation, you should have it dewormed at least twice a year with a broad-spectrum deworming agent.

Preventive de- worming

Therapeutic deworming is always indicated when you notice "worm symptoms."

Near the cat basket you will notice objects ranging in size from a grain of rice to a pumpkin seed. These are the dried-out segments of tapeworms. In addition, the cat suffers from diarrhea and extreme emaciation. The veterinarian can bring quick relief with a special tapeworm medication.

Symptoms of tapeworm infestation

With a heavy roundworm infestation, the cat's stool exhibits whitish, noodle-like, elongated structures. In this case the veterinarian will prescribe a special roundworm medication.

Symptoms of round- worm infestation

Fleas are extremely detrimental to the cat's health. They are intermediate hosts for tapeworms, and are responsible for anemia, itching, and allergy to fleas. Therefore, do not take the prevention of fleas lightly.

Fleas

Recognizing a flea infestation

Stand the cat on a white substrate, and comb it against the grain of the hair. Any black dots that appear on the substrate are flea feces. To be absolutely sure, sprinkle a little water on the dots. If they turn red, this indicates the presence of undigested blood in the flea feces.

Preventive measures against fleas

The best prevention against fleas is for the cat to wear a flea collar at all times. The collar must be replaced at regular intervals. There are shampoos, powders and sprays formulated for use on cats. Ask your ceterinarian which product(s) would be best for your animal.

A flea elimination program

By the time you notice fleas on your cat, you have a flea problem in your home. The only way to eliminate the problem is to eliminate the fleas—all of them. That means the fleas on your cat, the fleas in your home and, possibly, the fleas you may have in outdoor areas where your cat likes to spend time.

Fleas on your cat

Your veterinarian will recommend the appropriate shampoo, powder, spray or dip to use on your cat. There are formulations for older cats and kittens, with varying ingredients, and it's important to use the right product. Apply the recommended product to your kitten or cat following the directions exactly. This will kill the adult fleas on your cat, but will not prevent fleas in the house from jumping back on your cat, which is why you must move on to the rest of the house.

Adult fleas lay eggs on your cat that slide off the fur and onto whatever your cat touches, especially the places where your cat likes to sleep. Eggs can accumulate in the crevices of your cat's bed, between sofa cushions, in carpet fibers, on a pile of laundry, your child's bed—almost anywhere. To kill the egg stage, you will have to clean these spots thoroughly. Wash the cat bed, vacuum the carpets, launder anything the cat may have slept on. Your veterinarian can tell you which products are safe to spray on these areas, too.

Fleas in the house

Because outdoor cats are rarely confined like their canine cousins, they can pick up fleas almost anywhere. However, if there's a special spot your cat lounges in outdoors, and it's cushioned, treat it like an indoor spot by washing and spraying to kill eggs.

Fleas outdoors

While you are ridding your cat and home of fleas, you must be diligent about following up on the problem. After treating the cat, check it every day by combing with a special flea comb. Kill any fleas you find immediately.

Be diligent

Starting in the sixth year of life, cats need an annual veterinary checkup. The checkup consists of blood and urine tests, x-rays of the heart and lungs, and a thorough clinical examination of the four-legged friend by the veterinarian. By means of the laboratory tests, organic diseases can already be diagnosed at an early stage, long before the animal's owner notices symptoms.

Checkup at the veterinarian

Dental exam

To keep the gums and teeth healthy, the veterinarian must examine the cat's teeth at least once a year.

Ten tips for how you can keep the cat healthy

1. If you have a pedigreed cat, find out what diseases the breed is susceptible to. Have the veterinarian examine the cat regularly for these ailments.

2. Make sure the kitten receives vaccinations against infectious diseases, and is dewormed in a timely manner.

3. Combine the annual booster shots with a preventive veterinary checkup.

4. Do not try to accelerate the growth of your cat through too rich a diet.

5. In the course of daily care, check the skin, eyes, and ears.

6. Avoid overfeeding the cat.

7. Keep your cat's sleeping place and the food and water dishes meticulously clean.

8. Also, keep the cat itself very clean, and watch out for discharges in the anal and genital region.

9. Never let the cat outdoors at night, because they are more likely to be involved in a traffic accident or a fight.

10. Make sure that your cat gets enough exercise.

THE CAT AND THE VETERINARIAN

How many veterinarians should the cat have?

Ideally, a single veterinarian is sufficient to care for your cat throughout its life. In fact, the better the veterinarian knows your cat, the more quickly he will notice deviations from the normal state of health. The veterinarian will also recognize possible character traits of your pet, and can take them into account in his dealings with the cat. Furthermore, the veterinarian's records contain all the important information about your cat, such as vaccinations, dewormings, illnesses, laboratory results, and medications.

Choosing a veterinarian

If possible, choose a veterinarian near your home, to spare the cat from a long drive when it is sick. Make sure that the veterinarian is sympathetic to you and instills confidence in you. Watch to see if he handles his four-legged patients lovingly and patiently, because the cat notices, just as the human would, if it is being treated as an "important personality" or merely as "one patient among many."

THE CAT AND THE VETERINARIAN

**The first
visit to
the veteri-
narian**

Regardless of whether you have acquired a
kitten or an adult cat, take it as soon as
possible to the veterinarian you trust. In
this way, a timely plan for vaccinations
and deworming can be worked out, and the
cat and veterinarian can become acquainted in an undramatic situation.

**How often
should
the cat
see the
veteri-
narian?**

You should visit the veterinarian with your
cat at least once a year, both for the
purpose of the preventive veterinary
checkup and for the annual vaccinations.
Old cats must visit the veterinarian twice a
year.

**Should
the veteri-
narian
make a
house
call?**

Request a house call only if you have
absolutely no other choice. First, a house
call is considerably more expensive than
the same treatment at the office, and,
second, cats are usually far more disci-
plined at the veterinary clinic than in the
security of their familiar surroundings.
Furthermore, the lighting conditions in
private homes are usually inadequate for a
thorough examination. At the veterinary
clinic, the veterinarian also has access to
trained personnel and all the necessary
technical examination equipment. These
make it easier to diagnose the patient.

**The trip
to the
veteri-
narian**

Do not simply transport your cat to the
veterinarian in your arms. The cat could be
frightened by something and scratch you,
or even run away. Transport your cat exclusively in a securely closed pet carrier.
Plastic pet carriers are the best suited,
because you can clean and disinfect them
thoroughly. On the trip to the veterinarian,

many pussycats soil the cage with urine and feces. Less suitable are wicker pet carriers, because they are difficult to clean and disinfect. Another shortcoming of the wicker carrier is that kittens, in particular, readily chew through them. Also, do not take the cat out of the carrier in the waiting room, because it could be frightened or even bitten by a dog. Contact with other cats in the waiting room is not desirable either, because they could be sick and could infect your cat. Wait until you are in the treatment room before taking your cat from the carrier.

Always bring the cat's vaccination certificate. If the cat is taking medications, show them to the veterinarian. If you have noticed anything unusual in the cat's stool or vomit, bring a specimen of it.

What should you bring along?

Describe precisely to the veterinarian anything out of the ordinary you may have noticed with your cat recently. Information about changes in behavior is often just as important as the stool sample for the diagnosis. You should be able to answer the following questions: Does the cat eat with a good appetite? How much does it drink? Does it have diarrhea or constipation? Can it urinate and defecate at all? When was the last time it urinated or defecated? What is the appearance of the stool and urine with respect to color and consistency? Have you noticed blood in the urine and stool? Does the cat vomit more often than normal? What does the vomit look like, and at what intervals does it vomit? Does the

What will the veterinarian want to know?

cat cough, and how does the cough sound? Is the cat apathetic? Has it stopped grooming itself? Has it stopped using the litter box? Does it scratch a great deal? Does it scratch particularly at the ears? Does it shake its head frequently? Is the cat emaciated?

What will the cat have to put up with?

From the start, accustom your cat to certain hand holds that it will have to put up with during the veterinary examination.

It also should not be a problem with a cat to pull up the lips and to open the mouth. Without putting up too much of a struggle, the cat should allow the veterinarian to look in its ears and to examine its paws. You can practice all this in the course of caring for the cat.

IS MY CAT SICK?

Coughing

The cat — like the human being — has a cough center in the brain. This center can be reflexively stimulated by a variety of factors.

Coughing, triggered by a foreign body

When small foreign bodies get stuck in the throat, the windpipe, or the bronchia, the result is an intense dry cough. If the cat is unable to cough up the foreign body, the veterinarian must remove it. Some foreign bodies — particularly those in the bronchia — can only be detected with the aid of an x-ray.

Coughing, triggered by tonsillitis

Retching cough and the vomiting of white foam are indications of tonsillitis. In the healthy cat, the tonsils are retracted in pouches in the mucous membrane. In the case of severe tonsillitis, however, the tonsils become swollen and protrude from the pouches in the mucous membrane. The cat now thinks it has foreign bodies in its throat and tries to cough them up. You absolutely must visit the veterinarian, because chronic tonsillitis has a negative effect on the heart and joints.

Acute laryngitis	Symptoms of acute laryngitis include painful bouts of coughing. The causes include viral infections, the breathing in of noxious gases (for example, cigarette smoke), or simply too frequent meowing.
Coughing up mucus	The coughing up of mucus is a symptom of an acute infection of the bronchia.
Worm bronchitis	It is caused by roundworm larvae, which also infest the bronchia as they wander through the body.
Infectious bronchitis	It occurs as an accompanying symptom of infectious diseases.
What is the significance of sneezing?	When the cat sneezes, it can have many causes. The pussycat sneezes, for example, when it has inhaled a small foreign body and it gets stuck in the nose. Viral diseases that are accompanied by sniffling also make the cat sneeze. An allergy or a tumor in the nose also cause frequent sneezing.
When the cat pants	In this case you must go to the veterinarian immediately, because breathing through the mouth, that is panting, does not mean that the cat is hot. In the cat, panting indicates the presence of a serious, often life-threatening health disorder.
What is the significance of vomiting?	If the cat vomits up hair balls from time to time, it is harmless. If the cat vomits several times a day, however, this can have serious causes (for example, kidney failure, poisoning, viral infections). The cat absolutely must go to the veterinarian.

When cats suddenly drink excessively, it is a symptom of a serious health problem. The veterinarian must determine if the cause is diabetes (by no means rare in cats), an infection of the uterus, a hormonal disorder, or a dangerous kidney or liver disease.

When the cat drinks excessively

Excitement (for example, a visit to the veterinarian) stimulates a heavy flow of saliva in many cats. As a rule, this is harmless, and stops when the cat has calmed down again. When the cat salivates, however, and refuses to eat, this is a sign of a disease of the oral cavity, for example, painful gingivitis.

When the cat drools

If the cat has flatulence, but the feces are normal in color, the cause may simply be a faulty diet. A change in diet with more fiber and less meat will clear up the flatulence. If, however, lighter, clay-colored feces are present in addition to the flatulence, this indicates a disease of the pancreas.

What is the significance of flatulence?

If the entire urine is mixed with blood and is cherry red, this indicates a disease of the kidneys or poisoning. If there is dripping blood following urination, this is a symptom of an inflammation of the bladder or the ureter. In this case, make sure that the cat drinks plenty of fluids — possibly even weak tea.

What is the significance of blood in the urine?

If the urine is released only in a trickle, this is a symptom of an obstruction of the urethra by bladder stones or urinary calculus. Because a life-threatening uremia

What is the significance of trickling

123

urine?	can result from the backing up of the urine, the veterinarian must remove the stones or calculus as soon as possible.
Sudden unhouse-brokenness	The veterinarian must determine whether the cause is a psychological disorder or a physical disease.
Vigorous head-shaking	If the cat frequently scratches at its ears and frequently shakes its head vigorously, it probably is suffering from an infection of the ear canal. If the ear canal is also filled with a brownish-black discharge, the cat is infested with ear mites.
Head-tilting	This can be a symptom of a foreign body or a tumor in the ear.
When the cat has a swollen ear	Because of vigorous head shaking with an ear infection, a hematoma develops between the cartilage and skin of the ear. The ear flap appears as if inflated. The veterinarian must operate to remove the blood clot.
What is the signif-icance of itching?	Itching is always a symptom of a skin disease.
	• Itching and circular, hairless patches of skin indicate ringworm.
	• Itching in association with severe hair loss and scaly lesions indicates the presence of mange mites.
	• Severe itching over the entire body is often triggered by fleas and an allergy to fleas.

This is often a sign that a foreign body is stuck between the teeth. It can also be an indication, however, of painful gingivitis or a broken tooth.

Scratching at the muzzle

Although biting at the claws is part of the normal grooming behavior of the cat, if the cat bites at the claws constantly, this is an indication that a claw is either torn or ingrown. A thorough examination of the paw is necessary.

Excessive biting at the claws

In this case, the problem usually is conjunctivitis, caused by a draft or caustic cleaning agents, which irritate the eyes. With Persian Cats, blocked tear ducts are the cause of excessive tearing of the eyes.

When the eyes tear

A thick, pus-like eye discharge can be caused by conjunctivitis, an eye injury, or a viral infection (for example, infections of the upper respiratory tract). You should take a pus-like eye discharge seriously. Take the cat to the veterinarian as soon as possible.

Discharge of pus from the eyes

A protruding eyeball can be caused by a tumor behind the eye or the presence of glaucoma.

When the eyeball protrudes

Besides the upper and lower eyelid, cats have a third eyelid, the nicitating membrane, at the inner corner of the eye. Normally this lid is barely visible. When the nicitating membrane prolapses, it covers two-thirds of the eye. A prolapsed nicitating membrane always indicates a pathological condition. This can be poi-

Prolapsed nicitating membrane

soning, an infectious disease, a foreign body in the eye, or an injury to the eye. The ingestion of certain sedatives also causes the nicitating membrane to prolapse in cats.

Inability to defecate

Particularly with older cats, an incorrect diet and lack of exercise can lead to dreaded constipation. This can go so far that the animal cannot defecate at all. Then, so-called impacted feces form, which can lead to intestinal obstruction. Veterinary treatment is necessary.

Yellow coloration of the skin

This is a serious alarm signal! It usually indicates jaundice as a consequence of a serious liver disease or a disorder of the blood. The animal requires immediate veterinary treatment

Extreme paleness

Here, too, you must visit the veterinarian as soon as possible. Extreme paleness can be a symptom of anemia as well as life-threatening internal bleeding.

Dark coloration of the skin

As a consequence of chronic skin irritation, dark-colored to black patches often result. This is the case, for example, when the cat constantly gnaws on an area that itches. It is, so to speak, a kind of self protection by the skin — it thickens and darkens.

Lumps and tumors under the skin

Individual lumps and tumors of the skin are no reason for panic, because very often they are simply benign enlargements of the sebaceous glands or warts that require no treatment. Nevertheless, you should visit the veterinarian if you find a lump, because only he can determine whether a closer examination of the new growth is necessary. Particularly with older cats, you must consider that a tumor could be malignant.

When the cat suddenly develops a hemispherical, hot swelling, which is tough and hard at first, but becomes soft and elastic after a few days, it is probably an abscess. This is a collection of pus under the skin. The cause is usually a very small puncture wound, such as a bite suffered in a fight. An abscess must be drained by the veterinarian. **Hot, soft bulges in the skin**

This occurs only in unspayed female cats. The color of the discharge can be white, pink, yellow, or chocolate brown. The cause is an inflammation of the uterus. Immediate veterinary intervention is necessary. **Pus-like vaginal discharge**

Limping in a cat can have a number of causes: fractures, sprains, ligament damage, or congenital defects. Often, however, slight limping can be traced back simply to overexertion. In this case even an aspirin provides relief. To determine the cause, in any case you should take the cat to the veterinarian. **Limping**

With kittens, in particular, you must be prepared to visit the veterinarian at the slightest symptom of illness, because the little organism can become unbalanced in a very short time. **Alarm signals with kittens**

IS MY CAT SICK?

Alarm signals: A sudden change in temperament, apathy, the refusal of food and water, limping for no apparent reason and constantly whimpering quietly to itself, thick discharge from the eyes and nostrils, smelly ears, vomiting, and diarrhea are indications that you must bring the kitten to the veterinarian as soon as possible. Do not waste valuable time through senseless delay.

What is the correct way to treat a sick cat?

A sick cat needs plenty of rest. Never let it go outside, but rather confine the patient to a room that it is familiar with and in which it likes to stay. Provide it with a clean, warm, well-ventilated environment and a comfortable sick bed. It is important that the room is completely free of drafts. A basket with a raised rim or a shallow box with a comfortable cushion makes a suitable sick bed. Over the cushion put a waterproof oilcloth (sick cats often lose urine and feces!) and over that a washable cloth.

Should you force-feed your cat?

Sick cats usually have no appetite, but they can survive for many days without solid food. Therefore, force-feeding is usually unnecessary.

ADMINISTERING MEDICATION

When the four-legged patient refuses to take fluids and possibly also suffers from vomiting and diarrhea, it becomes dehydrated very quickly, which can lead to the cat's death. Therefore, it is necessary to administer fluids to sick cats. Well suited are defatted beef and chicken soup, because they simultaneously build up the cat's strength. To administer fluids, grasp the cat by the scruff of its neck and bend its head back. This causes the cat to open its mouth, so that you can drip the soup into the mouth with a spoon. You should not give more than one to two teaspoons at one time. You should, however, do this hourly if possible.

Administering fluids

• You can crush tablets that do not have a strong odor and mix them with a teaspoon of minced beef or canned food. Roll the mixture into a ball and give it to the hungry cat before feeding time.

Administering tablets

• This technique does not work with tablets that have a very strong odor (such as penicillin). To be able to administer such tablets, you must put the cat in your lap so that its face is turned away from you. Then, with your left hand, grasp the cat's head from behind and exert a slight pressure with your fingers behind the teeth. This causes the cat to open its mouth involuntarily. Now, with your right hand, you can push the tablet as far back on the tongue as possible. With the left hand hold the mouth shut, and with the right massage downward on the neck until you clearly feel the cat swallow the tablet. Another way to induce the cat to swallow the tablet is the following: tap your finger firmly on the cat's nose. This causes the cat to lick its nose and then automatically swallow.

Plastic pill dispenser

These are available on the market and from the veterinarian, and protect your fingers from painful bites.

Administering tablets to very uncooperative cats

Crush the tablet, mix it into a paste with water, and smear it on the paws. To clean itself, the cat will lick off the medicinal paste. Caution is needed here: with this method the cat may spit out some of the medicinal paste, making the dosage imprecise. This should be an absolute final resort.

Liquid medication

It is best to administer drops to the cat with a plastic syringe (without the needle!). Insert the syringe on the side of the mouth, behind the canine teeth, and inject the liquid very slowly into the oral cavity, so that the cat does not choke on it. Another method for administering liquid medication is the following: drip the medication onto the cat's paws. In most cases the cat will lick the medication from its paws.

A second person must hold the cat by the scruff of the neck. You yourself lubricate the pointed end of the suppository and lift the tail with one hand. With the other hand insert the suppository deeply into the anus. Then press the tail briefly against the anus, so that the patient cannot immediately squeeze the suppository out again.

Administering supposi- tories

First, you must clean the eye with a wad of cotton wool soaked in chamomile tea. Important: Always clean from the outside corner of the eye in toward the nose! Hold the cat's head firmly by the scruff of the neck, and simultaneously pull down the lower lid with your thumb. With the other hand, drip the eyedrops into the pocket between the lid and eye.

Drip eyedrops into the eye

First, clean the eye as above. Hold the cat's head firmly from behind, and simultaneously pull down the lower lid with your thumb. A second person now squeezes an approximately one-centimeter-long bead of ointment into the pocket between the lid and eye. Now draw the upper and lower lid over the bead of ointment to carefully distribute the ointment in the eye.

Admini- stering eye ointment

Hold the tip of the cat's ear and lift it up to expose the ear canal. Then insert the tip of the plastic ear-drop bottle as deeply into the ear canal as possible and give the bottle a good squeeze. It is impossible to count the number of ear drops; it is also unnec-

Ear drops

essary. A little too much is better than too little. Finally, massage the cartilage below the ear opening up and down. This produces a sloshing sound, which indicates that the ear drops are being distributed throughout the ear canal.

Rubbing with liquids

Always rub in liquids against the grain of the hair, because this is the only way to reach the skin, where, of course, the liquids are supposed to take effect. With long-haired cats, you must part the hair repeatedly to get the liquid to the skin.

Ointments

The use of ointments is problematic with cats, because cats — driven by their cleaning instinct — will immediately lick them off. If the use of ointments is unavoidable, you must apply a bandage over them.

Bandages

If the cat tries to pull the bandage off, stick it to the coat with wide strips of cellophane tape. If the cat then continues to tug at the bandage, it automatically pulls on its own hair, which hurts. In this way, the animal soon learns that it must leave the bandage alone. At the proper time, the veterinarian will then carefully remove the bandage with curved scissors.

DANGER OF INFECTION BY THE CAT

In principle, all animals can be infected with toxoplasmosis, but not all animals can transmit it.

Toxo-plasmosis

Toxoplasmosis in the cat usually produces only mild symptoms, much like those of a cold. Rarely it cause seizures, which can be confused with epilepsy.

How is toxo-plasmosis expressed?

House cats become infected by eating raw meat. Cats that are allowed to go outdoors can become infected by prey animals or the feces of stray cats.

How does the cat become infected?

Humans can become infected by the careless handling of cat feces. The most frequent source of infection of humans, however, is food. The disease is almost always transmitted through the consumption of raw or insufficiently cooked meat.

How do humans become infected?

Dogs cannot transmit the pathogen to humans, because they do not shed the pathogens with their feces.

Dogs

DANGER OF INFECTION BY THE CAT

Is toxo-plasmosis dangerous? Toxoplasmosis need not necessarily be dangerous. Seventy percent of the population has survived an infection during their lives, without even having been aware of it.

When is toxo-plasmosis dangerous? Toxoplasmosis is dangerous to pregnant women, because the pathogen can injure the unborn child. Therefore, routine blood tests — toxoplasmosis tests — are performed on the fetus in the first three months of pregnancy.

What about the toxo-plasmosis test? The level of the antibody titer determines whether the result is positive. If it is normal, the mother had previously been infected with toxoplasmosis, and there is no further danger for mother or child.

If the test shows a very high titer, however, a second test must be performed after two weeks. If the titer has not risen, there is no acute infection. Otherwise, the disease must be treated with antibiotics to protect the unborn child from harm.

Prevention of toxo-plasmosis The following measures are recommended to women for the prevention of toxo plasmosis: Do not eat any raw meat (steak tartare)! Do not feed any raw meat to cats living in the household! Practice meticulous hygiene when cleaning the litter box! To give away the four-legged friend, out of fear of infection, would be totally pointless.

Rabies Rabies is caused by a virus that causes severe inflammation of the central nervous system and ultimately leads to death. The principal carrier and principal vector of the virus is the red fox. The percentage of rabid cats fortunately is very low.

The disease is transmitted through contact with the saliva of rabid animals when they bite. The rabies virus cannot penetrate unbroken skin. Bites through clothing are less serious, because the textile fibers have a certain filtering effect.

Only cats that go outdoors have the opportunity to be infected with rabies. The infection is primarily transmitted through the bites of infected wild animals. House cats that never go outdoors are not at risk for rabies.

How does the cat become infected?

From the time of infection to the outbreak of the disease, there is an incubation period of two to eight weeks. The first symptoms of illness are changes in behavior (for example, shy animals suddenly become confiding and vice versa), and the dilation and fixation of the pupils. Later, the animals salivate a great deal and become aggressive. In the final stages the animal becomes paralyzed. The hoarse and finally toneless screeching is conspicuous, which is caused by the advanced paralysis of the larynx. Unfortunately, rabid cats have a tendency to jump in people's faces — and the closer the injury is to your brain, the greater is the threat to life. You must keep in mind, however, that every aggressive cat that has gone wild does not necessarily have rabies. A mother cat

How is rabies expressed in the cat?

defending its kittens can also react in this way.

Prevention of rabies

Since rabies is also life-threatening for humans, you absolutely must have your cat — even if it goes outdoors only occasionally — vaccinated against rabies. The basic immunization consists of two vaccinations at an interval of three weeks. An annual booster shot is necessary. Only house cats, that absolutely never go outdoors, do not need to be vaccinated against rabies.

Because a vaccinated cat itself cannot be infected with rabies, it is also impossible for it to transmit rabies to other living creatures.

Your cat has bitten someone

If your cat has been vaccinated properly against rabies, show the vaccination certificate to the injured person and the attending doctors. This calms down the person who was bitten, and in many cases spares him from the postexpositional rabies vaccination.

An unvaccinated cat has bitten someone

If a human being has been bitten, it is important to wash out the wound immediately with plenty of soap and water, and to treat it with a disinfectant (70-percent alcohol, tincture of iodine). Then the person must go to the doctor immediately.

A strange cat has bitten

If the cat that has bitten was able to get away without having been identified beforehand, the bitten person must begin the

postexpositional rabies vaccination immediately.

someone

This is the vaccination that is administered to people following injury by a rabid
animal, or one that is suspected of being
rabid. This protective measure must take
place as soon as possible. The first vaccination following a bite consists of two
injections, one in the left, and one in the
right upper arm. The second series of
injections takes place two weeks later, and
the third two weeks after that. With very
serious bites, the doctor additionally sprays
the wound with immune serum (complete
antibodies).

*What is
the
postex-
positional
vacci-
nation?*

Anyone who feels in danger can get protection. The basic immunization consists of
two vaccinations, with the second given 28
days after the first. The first booster shot is
administered 6 to 12 months later. Additional booster shots are required every five
years.

*Preventive
vaccination
for rabies
in
humans*

The rabies vaccination is completely harmless, because the vaccine is a dead vaccine.
This means that it contains only killed
viruses, which cannot produce any symptoms of disease.

*Is the
rabies
vaccination
dangerous?*

The cat itself does not become ill from
Lymphoreticulosis benigna, because it is
only a carrier. The disease is transmitted to
humans by cats through scratches and
bites. The incubation period from the time
of infection until the outbreak of the illness is three to fourteen days. Initially,

*Lympho-
reticulosis
benigna*

the injured place on the skin becomes inflamed, and subsequently there is swelling, and festering of the affected lymph nodes. Occasionally, fever and chills are accompanying symptoms. The illness usually clears up without complications.

Salm- onella

Salmonella causes severe, feverish diarrhea and vomiting. In principle, transmission is possible from cats to humans. The cat usually becomes affected from eating infected, incompletely cooked meat. Cats that go outside can also become infected from eating mice or birds. Never feed your cat raw meat!

Scabies

This condition is caused by microscopically small parasites: scabies mites. The cat suffers from intense itching and severe hair loss. Pustules and finally crusty scabs develop.

Can a cat with scabies infect humans?

Sometimes humans who have close contact with cats infected with scabies develop itchy nodules on the torso and arms. We should not confuse these skin manifestations, however, with true human scabies, because the scabies mites of the cat cannot survive and reproduce on humans. The nodules they produce disappear on their own in three to four weeks, whereas human scabies requires more intensive therapy.

Ringworm

Unfortunately, ringworm occurs relatively frequently in cats. Because the ringworm fungus can be transmitted from the cat to humans, it is particularly important to recognize ringworm on your four-legged friend as soon as possible. In the cat, ringworm occurs most frequently on the head and legs. Circular, hairless lesions, broken hairs, as well as scaling and reddening of the skin are alarm signals that require an immediate trip to the veterinarian. With severely affected cats, the hair becomes covered with such heavy encrustations that you can even see them with the naked eye. Itching can occur, but is not always present.

How do humans become infected?

If the veterinarian has made the diagnosis of "ringworm," you must disinfect the cat's environment throughly. The reason for this, is that humans can be infected not just through direct contact with the cat, but also through objects such as brushes, combs, blankets, upholstery, dandruff, hair, and so forth. It is essential to keep the cat's environment as clean as possible, because ringworm spores can remain viable for years in a dry environment.

Worms

Many cat owners are afraid of being infected with worms by their cat. Therefore, it is important to have the veterinarian explain how to control worms on the first visit. Furthermore, at the slightest suspicion of a worm infestation you should visit the veterinarian immediately, to prevent the propagation of the parasites through timely treatment. It is possible today to control successfully all the kinds of worms affecting cats with a single broad-spectrum deworming agent. The deworming of the kitten, and subsequently the regular preventive deworming of the adult cat, is a matter of course.

Round-worms

When your cat has roundworms, you will usually notice it by the worms that are spontaneously passed with the stool or vomited up. Kittens frequently are infected with roundworms, because they already become infected during the nursing period through the mother's milk. The poor kittens then tend to suffer from weight loss, rachitic disorders, diarrhea, and rough coat.

Can round-worms infect humans?

In theory, humans can be infected while playing and cuddling with cats infected with worms, because in 90 percent of all cats infected with roundworms, invisible roundworm eggs cling to the coat.

Are round-worms dangerous for humans?

No! They are not dangerous since the roundworm eggs that are taken up by humans cannot develop normally, because a human is an unsuitable host. The infection usually runs its course without symptoms. Only in exceptional cases does the infestation lead to slight fever, and rarely impaired vision.

Preventing infection

Besides the regular deworming of the kitten, strict hygienic guidelines are helpful: Keep your cat's bed clean, and bathe the cat to remove any roundworm eggs that may be clinging to the coat.

Tape-worms

All kinds of tapeworms need an intermediate host, which is then eaten by the final host — thus, the cat. The kind of tapeworm species that will infect our four-legged

friend, therefore, depends on which intermediate host it has access to.

This occurs primarily in cats that spend
much time outdoors and like to hunt. For
its development, it requires the mouse or
rat as the intermediate host. The virulent
worms develop in the liver of the intermediate host. The cat becomes infected with
the feline tapeworm when it eats the mouse
or rat. You can tell if a cat is infected by the
moving, white tapeworm segments in the
cat's stool.

*The
typical
feline
tapeworm*

Because this tapeworm requires the flea
as the intermediate host for its development, it occurs both in cats and dogs.
The pumpkinseed-shaped tapeworm segments with the eggs and pass out of the
cat's body with the stool. These cling to
the cat's coat and are taken up by the
fleas. If the flea now bites the cat, it
becomes infected with the tapeworm. A
heavy infestation leads to stomach ache,
diarrhea, emaciation, and anemia. An
occasional infection of humans with the
pumpkinseed-like tapeworm is possible.
Symptoms similar to those of the cat are
exhibited. This is unpleasant, but not
dangerous.

If you suspect the presence of tapeworms,
bring your cat to the veterinarian immediately. By examining the stool, he can determine the type of tapeworm and treat the
cat with appropriate medication.

*What if
you
suspect
tape-
worms?*

ALLERGIES

What are allergies? — Allergies are hypersensitive reactions to various substances in the environment. Allergy sufferers are especially sensitive to substances they inhale. Such inhaled allergens include, for example, the pollen of grasses and trees, dust mites, animal hairs, the tiniest flakes of animal skin, and so forth.

Can you be allergic to several substances? — Yes, the majority of allergy sufferers react positively to several substances on allergy tests. Not all substances tested as allergy triggers, however, always provoke symptoms of illness.

Allergy to cats — Because cat hair and dandruff number among the inhaled allergens, an "allergy to cats" produces the same symptoms as allergies to pollen or dust mites, namely, watery, swollen eyes, runny nose, and sometimes even asthma.

Should you give the cat away? — No! Because most allergies are multifactorial — that is, they are caused simultaneously by various substances — giving the cat away will not help matters.

• The bedroom must always be free of allergens. Therefore, do not let the cat in.

• Vacuum the cat regularly with the vacuum cleaner on its lowest setting. The cat will gradually become used to it.

• Bathe or wash the cat once a week. Many cats are regular water rats, and even like to bathe.

• Always clean the house thoroughly!

• The "Outright Allergy Remedy," which is a liquid that you rub into the cat's coat twice a week, has proved to be very effective. This liquid reduces human allergic reactions to cat allergens.

• Try the so-called desensitization therapy. This is a series of injections that must be carried out over two to three years.

The right way to proceed with allergies to cats

SEXUALITY

Sexual maturity
• Normal house cats generally become sexually mature at six to seven months of age, in some cases somewhat earlier.

• Pedigreed cats are late maturing, and do not reach sexual maturity until nine to twelve months of age.

Estrus, or the heat
As a sign of sexual maturity, female cats go in heat. The cat in heat eats less, writhes on the floor, and calls incessantly for a mate.

Duration of the heat
Normally, the heat lasts two to seven days. A house cat that does not encounter a tomcat during estrus can go into a state of "permanent heat," which of course is extremely unpleasant for both the animal and the owner.

What is "permanent heat"?
In cats, ovulation takes place only during the act of mating. If mating does not take place, the sexual cycle is blocked, and the cat lapses into the permanent heat.

Do old cats go in heat?
Yes! Unspayed cats go in heat until an advanced age and can also still get pregnant.

Cats go in heat two to three times a year, and can get pregnant any time they go in heat.

How often is heat?

You can suppress the heat by means of hormonal preparations in the form of pills ("cat pills") or injections, and can prevent it through spaying.

How can you suppress the heat?

The pill is not recommended as a permanent solution for cats, because with long-term use it can lead to a dangerous infection of the uterus. In extreme cases, the animal's death can only be prevented by a complete hysterectomy.

"Cat pills"

Spaying the female cat is still the best method for preventing unwanted offspring. Because animal shelters are overcrowded and it is hard to find people willing to adopt a pet, you should have your female cat spayed as early as possible.

Spaying the female cat

Under full anesthesia, both ovaries and a part of the uterus are removed.

What happens?

Normal house cats should not be spayed before six months of age, and pedigreed cats not before nine months of age. If the first heat occurs earlier, however, the cat can also be spayed earlier.

How old for spaying?

In the vernacular, the spaying of the female cat is often incorrectly called "sterilization." In sterilization, however, only the fallopian tubes are tied, the heat and false pregnancy still occur. For these reasons, sterilization is not customarily performed on the female cat.

Sterilization

SEXUALITY

Does spaying also have drawbacks for the female cat?

No, on the contrary, spaying even has benefits for the health of the female cat: Spayed cats neither develop infections of the uterus nor tumors of the mammary glands. Spaying also does not cause any negative changes in behavior. In fact, the female cat usually becomes even more affectionate and even-tempered.

Signs of sexual maturity in the tomcat

The sexually mature tomcat instinctively sprays its urine mixed with scent throughout the home — on the floor, furniture, and walls — to mark its territory. Some of the other behavior patterns of the sexually mature tomcat are the grabbing by the scruff of the neck and the jumping on other animals. It is also willing to roam for miles in search of a female cat in heat.

Neutering of the tomcat

Because any unneutered tomcat can contribute to the birth of numerous unwanted kittens, we must recommend to every owner of a tomcat to have this minor operation carried out on his or her pet.

What happens during neutering?

Under full anesthesia, the testicles are removed. The small incision that is made does not even require stitches. In most cases, the four-legged friend is up and about again the same day.

At what age may the tomcat be neutered?

In no case should you have the operation performed before the end of the sixth month of life. In any case, you should wait until the urogenital system is fully developed, which does not happen with some animals until the ninth or tenth month. In any case, pedigreed tomcats may not be neutered until after the ninth month of life.

No, as long as you do not overfeed them, neutered tomcats do not become obese. Overweight is always the result of over-feeding!

Are they obese?

Following neutering, the tomcat is more lovable, even-tempered, affectionate, and cleaner. Another benefit: It no longer roams as far.

Benefits of neutering

BREEDING CATS

Are there takers for the offspring? This is the important question to ask before you decide to breed your cat. The misery of cats is already great enough! If you cannot resolve this question, then have your cat neutered from the start.

Must the cat bear a litter? It is an old superstition that it is important for the cat's health to have kittens at least once in its life. In reality, this plays absolutely no role.

Sexual maturity Sexual maturity is the time when the female cat may be mated for the first time. Although stray female cats as a rule are mated in their first heat, you should prevent this with your cat, because it is not truly sexually mature until it is at least one year old.

Partner selection When you have come to the conclusion after careful consideration that your completely normal house cat should have kittens, simply put it together with an unneutered male during the heat. It will certainly be mated. If you are the owner of a pedigreed cat, however, inquire with the association of breeders for your particular breed. They will supply you with a list of eligible studs.

Sometimes this is necessary with pedigreed cats, when the chosen tomcat and the female do not get along and refuse to mate.

Artificial insemination

• Pink color of the teats: In the third to fourth week of pregnancy, the teats turn pink and begin to become erect.

Signs of pregnancy

• Weight gain: The cat gradually gains two to five pounds, depending on how many kittens it is carrying.

• The belly gets rounder: Do not try to feel the kittens by pressing on the belly. They could be injured!

• Change in behavior: The female cat becomes even more affectionate, and with time also less active.

At the 20th day after mating, the veterinarian can determine by examining the vagina, and with ultrasound, if the cat is pregnant. The veterinarian can also detect the embryo by abdominal palpation. At the 45th day, the number of kittens can be determined on an x-ray.

Confirming pregnancy

Pregnancy lasts an average of 63 days. The kittens, however, can also arrive several days earlier or later. This is dependent on

Duration of pregnancy

149

the breed and litter size. Large litters have a shorter, small litters a longer, gestation period.

Litter size Pedigreed cats usually have smaller litters than do normal house cats.

The nutrition of the pregnant cat In the first three weeks of pregnancy, feed your cat as usual. Only then does the cat need more food, which you should feed it in several small portions spread out over the day. Because the pregnant cat needs more vitamins and minerals, have your veterinarian prescribe a suitable preparation for you.

Where should the cat give birth? Because cats pick out their own place to give birth, in any case, offer several places for the maternity box. The location must be in a quiet, secluded corner of the home — away from the daily hubbub and naturally out of drafts. Put the maternity box in the place the cat prefers. Start getting the cat accustomed to the maternity box during pregnancy.

Maternity box A sturdy cardboard box or a wooden box make suitable maternity boxes. The maternity box should have dimensions of approximately 12 x 20 inches. The sides should be at least 8 inches high. In any case, it must be long enough that the cat can stretch out inside it. It must not be too large either, however, because the female should be able to support its legs against the sides of the box during labor.

On a firm pillow with a waterproof cover, place a thick layer of newspaper. On top of the newspaper, spread towels or cloth diapers. It is ideal to install an infrared lamp 36 inches above the maternity box.

Furnishing the maternity box

Just before delivery, the cat becomes increasingly restless, inspects the maternity box, and leaves it again. With many — but not all — cats the body temperature falls about 24 hours before delivery. The vulva becomes swollen and gives off a slimy-watery secretion. Intensive licking of the vulva, and finally the labor pains, announce the onset of birth.

When does birth begin?

Although cats have very easy births and only rarely need veterinary help, they appreciate the presence of their "own" person at the birth. Stroke your cat gently — this comforts it and simultaneously massages the body.

Should you stay with your cat?

An average cat birth lasts three to six hours. Sometimes, however, it can take up to two days before all the kittens are born.

How long does birth last?

The interval between the birth of the individual kittens varies from five minutes to an hour.

Each kitten is born inside a protective amniotic sac. The mother cat bites it open. Then the mother severs the umbilical cord just above the belly. Attached to the umbilical cord is the afterbirth, which the mother eats. Do not prevent the mother cat

What happens to the afterbirth?

from eating the afterbirth, because it contains valuable hormones that promote milk production.

Litter size An average litter contains three to six kittens, rarely up to ten.

When should you assist? Especially with first-time mother cats, it sometimes happens that they forget to bite open the amniotic sac and to bite through the umbilical cord. In this case you must provide assistance. Pick up the newborn, tear open the amniotic sac and pull it off the kitten. Gently massage the newborn to stimulate the breathing reflex. Then tie off the umbilical cord lightly with a thread, and cut it behind the thread. Then return the newborn to the mother immediately, to avoid disrupting the mother-kitten relationship.

When must you call the veterinarian?

• When the gestation period exceeds 66 days, you should call in the veterinarian.

• If no kittens have been born two to three hours after the start of labor, veterinary assistance is necessary.

• If, two to three hours after the normal birth of one or more kittens, no more kittens have been born, the veterinarian must intervene.

• If very large-headed kittens are expected — for example, with Persians — you should consult the veterinarian from the start.

Because the flow of milk begins before—at the latest, during—birth, the first kittens already start to nurse while the mother is still bringing more kittens into the world.

When do the kittens begin to nurse?

At an age of three to four weeks you can start adding solid food to the diet. Canned kitten food is well suited because its mineral content meets the increased requirement during the growth phase. You can also feed fresh minced meat or finely chopped, cooked chicken.

When should you begin feeding solid food?

As soon as you begin feeding the kittens solid food, you must make drinking water available to them.

Depending on how many kittens there are, the nursing cat needs two to three times more food than a cat that is not nursing. Spread out this larger amount of food over six meals a day.

Nutrition of the nursing mother

Kittens come into the world blind and deaf. In the second week of life, they open their eyes and raise their ears, and begin to see and hear.

When do kittens see and hear?

At eight weeks of age, kittens are weaned from their mother's milk.

When are kittens weaned?

If the mother cat has no milk or has even died, you must raise the young kittens with a mother-milk substitute. You can buy this formula milk from the veterinarian or in the pet store.

If the cat has no milk

Up to an age of three weeks, you must feed orphaned kittens every three hours.

How should you feed formula?

You can feed the formula milk in a baby bottle for kittens. With very weak kittens, try it with an eyedropper or a plastic syringe.

Weight gain

Kittens must gain at least one-half ounce a day.

Essential: stimulating urination and defecation

Up to an age of about three weeks, the young kittens cannot urinate and defecate on their own. These functions normally are stimulated by the licking of the belly and anus by the mother. If the mother has died, you must massage the belly and anus of the kitten with a moist wad of cotton wool, to stimulate excretion.

THE OLD CAT

Thanks to vaccination, preventive check-ups, and proper nutrition, cats, too, are living longer and longer today. Twenty-year-old cats are no longer a rarity today.

What is "aging"?

"Aging" absolutely is not a disease. It does mean, however, that the powers of regeneration, thus the renewal of all the cells in the body, diminish. As a result, the efficiency of the organs naturally also decreases. Furthermore, in old age the cat is more susceptible to diseases, because the effectiveness of the immune system diminishes.

We can say that a cat is old starting at an age of approximately ten years.

When is a cat old?

Physical and psychological stress clearly can shorten the life of an old cat. For example, older cats cope poorly with a change of location. Constant noise and commotion in a previously quiet place can put the cat under constant stress, and thereby shorten its life. An old cat also no longer tolerates a move as well as a younger cat.

What shortens the life of the old cat?

THE OLD CAT

How is old age expressed? Signs of old age in the cat include problems with the joints, an inelastic spine, blunt claws, a scaly nose, as well as problems with the teeth and gums. Furthermore, the activity of the old cat decreases. It changes its habits — for example, it sleeps more than before — and behavior, and forgets acquired behavior patterns. In other words, it becomes "senile." One of the changes is, for example, that previously housebroken cats suddenly become unhousebroken again. The movements of the old cat become slower, and it becomes more sensitive to heat and cold than before. Old cats often become conspicuously emaciated, as well.

White hair? Old cats at most get a few white hairs on the face.

Health disorders As with humans, with the cat, as well, there are health disorders that appear with greater frequency in old age.

Thirst decreases In old cats the thirst reflex is even less developed than in young cats. Therefore, they usually drink much too little. This leads to the general dehydration of the tissues. This also reduces the kidney function, and the detoxification of the body no longer functions as well. For this reason, always encourage your old four-legged friend to drink. Old cats that drink little water often readily drink defatted soup or the meat water left over from thawing frozen meat. You can also mix plenty of lukewarm liquid with the food.

When the old cat no longer smells and tastes properly, it accordingly eats less. Therefore, offer the old cat particularly tasty food and warm it slightly. You can also feed it special "senior diets."

The senses of smell and taste diminish

Older cats no longer see as acutely as before. Sometimes old cats even become completely blind. Then it is essential always to put the food dish in exactly the same place, and always to arrange the furniture in exactly the same way, so the blind cat can orient itself. Also consider that things that are completely harmless for a sighted cat, such as a fire in an open fireplace, can be life-threatening for a blind cat.

Eyesight diminishes

When old cats no longer hear well, clogged ear canals are not to blame, but rather the degeneration of the cochlea and the bones of the middle ear. You can provide the cat with slight improvement by giving it regular supplements of vitamins B12, B1, B6, and E under your veterinarian's supervision.

Hearing diminishes

Many older cats have problems with their digestion. Therefore, keep a close eye on the litter box and watch for alarm signals. These include, for example, when the cat spends more time than usual in the litter box, when the cat scatters the cat litter all over the room, when the stool becomes harder and drier, and when the cat has pain and screeches while defecating. If you observe any of these symptoms, you should add something to the

Constipation

food that will make the stool softer, such as two teaspoons of melted butter or bran at every meal.

Impacted feces

Constipation in older cats can go so far that the cat is no longer able to defecate at all. When this is the case, so-called impacted feces form. The cat stops eating and vomits repeatedly. The anus becomes reddened and inflamed. As therapy, the veterinarian must administer special injections to stimulate the bowel. If these do not help, the veterinarian must remove the impacted feces under anesthesia.

Problems with the teeth and gums

Older cats, in particular, are more likely to get tartar. Particularly on the molars, you often find a thick buildup of tartar. This tartar can lead to infected roots, which in turn can cause inflammation of the oral cavity and the tonsils. Abscesses can also develop. Furthermore, tartar can also lead to painful gingivitis, which keeps the cat from eating. Therefore, it is very important to have the veterinarian remove the tartar in time.

Why do cats become "stiff" with age?

After resting for a while, old cats move very stiffly and slowly at first. The more the cat then moves, the better it will warm up. To blame for this "stiff-leggedness" is arthritis, that is, age-related degeneration of the joints.

How can you help a "stiff"

Cover the cat while sleeping, because warmth is beneficial with arthritis. Hot-water bottles and electric blankets, on a low setting, help arthritic cats. Definitely visit the veterinarian, as well, because injections can ease the pain and stop the progress of the arthritis.

cat?

Because old cats are no longer as flexible, they can no longer clean themselves as thoroughly as in their younger days. Consequently, the coat no longer shines as beautifully as before and becomes somewhat rough. Therefore, take plenty of time to care for your old cat. It will reward you for it with a longer life. Now brush even your short-haired cat daily. This not only produces a beautiful coat, it simultaneously stimulates the circulation. Also, talk lovingly and frequently to your old four-legged friend.

Old cats require more care

Even with the most indulgent and best of care, there comes the day when the veterinarian tells you that your pet's quality of life has fallen to minimum, and can no longer be justified because of its suffering. He will also advise you that further treatment will not extend life, but rather only prolong death. Then you should end the animal's suffering by consenting to having the cat put to sleep (euthanized). The cat is put to sleep by means of an injection, which is completely painless. Stay with your friend until its last breath, talk to it, and caress it. Then it will gently go to sleep.

When is it time to say goodbye?

There are symptoms that will tell you that the cat probably can no longer be saved:

How you can tell when the

159

cat can no longer be saved

• Confusion: The cat can no longer orient itself, and can no longer find, for example, the litter box or its basket.

• Extreme weakness: It stumbles while walking, leans against something out of sheer weakness, or breaks down before reaching its destination.

• The cat remains lying or sitting in the litter box.

• The cat sits in front of the water dish and lets its head hang in it.

• Infusions under the skin are no longer absorbed.

• The body temperature is below the normal value: You can tell this by the extremely cold ears and paws.

• Heavy breathing (panting) through the open mouth.

What happens after the cat is put to sleep?

If you notice symptoms of this kind with your old and sick cat, you should not be surprised if your veterinarian advises you to have it put to sleep.

Depending on your own feelings, you can leave the dead animal in the clinic, bury it in a pet cemetery, or have it cremated.